MARGARET M. COFFIN, an acknowl-
edged authority on American antiques
specializing in tinware, is the author of
numerous articles in periodicals and the
coauthor of a two-volume compendium on
painted tinware. DEATH IN EARLY
AMERICA is her first book for the popular
market.

Married and the mother of four grown
sons, Mrs. Coffin is a member of several
antiquarian societies, has been a teacher
and a textbook editor, and lectures on her
specialty to historical and folklore societies.
She enjoys collecting antiques and restoring
them when necessary, and she is a gifted
amateur photographer. She and her husband live in an old farmhouse near Northville, New York.

DEATH IN

EARLY AMERICA

The History and Folklore of
Customs and Superstitions of Early
Medicine, Funerals, Burials, and Mourning

by MARGARET M. COFFIN

THOMAS NELSON INC., PUBLISHERS

Nashville   New York

First edition

Library of Congress Cataloging in Publication Data
Coffin, Margaret M.
    Death in early America.
    Bibliography: p.
    Includes index.
    1. Funeral rites and ceremonies—United States—
History. 2. Death. 3. Folk medicine—United States—
History. I. Title.
GT3203.C63   393   76-7513
ISBN 0-8407-6482-0

SACRED TO
the
MEMORY
OF

Maude Fuller
and
Bert Job Mattison

Loving, strong,
Hardworking –
'From the old school'
They were the backbone
of a town, and
of their children.

ACKNOWLEDGMENTS

Many people have helped with this volume. The person who has helped the most, though, is my husband, Charles, who is responsible for most of the photography not otherwise identified. He has also lent a perceptive editorial ear. Others who read part of the manuscript and made suggestions were Jeff, Candy, and Duke Coffin, Ann and Berwyn Mattison, Bernie and Budd Knight. Pris Griffith and Pat Tocatlian sent me newspaper clippings. Nellie Ryan put the bibliography together. Denise Davis, while a student at Burnt Hills High School, sorted folklore materials and typed them. Candy Coffin selected the remedies and epitaphs for Chapters 11 and 12 and—bless her sweet, generous soul— typed for me.

For sending photographs for illustrations or allowing us to photograph pieces in their collections, I am particularly grateful to Mr. William O. Hickok, V, from the William Penn Memorial Museum, Harrisburg, Pennsylvania; Virginia Gunter and Renee Klish Ginsberg from Old Museum Village, Monroe, New York; Amy Bess Miller and John H. Ott from Hancock Shaker Village, Pittsfield, Massachusetts; Mr. and Mrs. Claude Lipe, Northville, New York; Martha Blazer from the Kentucky Historical Society, Frankfort, Kentucky; Mary Lou Vineyard and Sue Durn from the New York State Historical Association at Cooperstown, New York; Barbara Evans and Maureen Ahearn from the Albany

ACKNOWLEDGMENTS

Institute of History and Art in Albany, New York; and Mr. William H. Seeger from the Old Stone Fort, Schoharie, New York.

I am also grateful to the many folklore-class students who helped by contributing to the list of cures in Chapter 11, among them Donna Aubrey, Jim Cech, Liz Curran, Holly Curwen, Holly Freiburghouse, Laurie Garrison, Jeff Henry, Kathy Isabella, Diane Jezierski, Grace Loomis, Kathy Loukes, Rod Lowell, Denise Marquette, Tom Mitchell, Steve Ott, Ellen Radtke, Wendy Safford, Betty Santeler, Tracy Scrafford, Dona Sherman, and Karen Willyoung.

Other students made generous contributions to the section on epitaphs in Chapter 12. They are: Carolyn E. Sullivan, Craig V. Cary, Tom Nielsen, Babette Horan, and Karen Rohling. I am grateful to them all.

CONTENTS

AUTHOR'S NOTE

This is not a morbid book. Nor is it intended to be an irreverent one. The decision to start research for it was certainly influenced by happenings in my own life. As a student of folklore, I grew curious as I learned more of the history of American customs surrounding death, its causes, its ceremonies, its traditions.

We are all curious about death, and each of us, probably, has investigated his own attitude toward it. Religion directs the way some of us look upon death, but it is not the answer for all.

Incidents that occurred while I was working on this volume have sometimes left me wondering whether I should laugh or cry. For example, I heard about two elderly sisters. One was too close when she stoked up the woodburning potbelly in their home; her apron caught fire and she died of burns. That night her sister mused: "You know, Sister was cold all day. I was busy putting wood on the fire, and I just couldn't get her warmed up. . . . I guess she's warm enough now."

I found the cemeteries I visited among the most peaceful places I've been. The atmosphere prevailing was one of love, not mourning, and I gained a genuine admiration for the imagination and artistry of the stonecutters who had spent hours carefully ornamenting grave markers, perhaps signing their names or initials with pride. The memorials, though sometimes too senti-

mental, range in execution from quaintly primitive to remarkably
skillful, and they show a sincerity that is affecting.

Research for this volume has led down many paths. Along
with relevant material, I've discovered all sorts of odd bits. For
instance, did you know that the real way to pick out a witch, if
one happens to be in a room crowded with people, is to look
through a knothole cut from a coffin? Also, are you aware that
around Keller, Illinois, everyone digs in, literally, when someone
dies? Even today grave digging there is a voluntary community
effort. And—watch out for this one—there's an old superstition
that it is fatal to "let a lizard count your teeth"!

The material for this book has come from personal observation;
from bona fide histories of undertaking; from stories told to me
by acquaintances and by students in my folklore classes; from
informal, intimate written histories and reminiscences; and from
the "Yankee Yarns" of Alton Blackington, veteran storyteller
over popular Boston radio station WBZ. The latter were provided
on tape by John Furman, a former folklore student. More material came from original sources—letters, ledgers, and daybooks.
Much of the information in Chapter 3, on warnings of imminent
death, and in Chapter 7, which deals with epitaphs, was gathered
by students in Burnt Hills-Ballston Lake High School, Burnt
Hills, New York. The material in Chapters 11 and 12, "Some
Early Cures and Remedies" and "Epitaphs," was collected almost
in its entirety by these same students. I am especially grateful to
these young men and women, who happened to share one of my
particular interests.

Perhaps, among all of these sources, some are suspect. It would
be impossible to find written verification for all of the stories.
The book, therefore, becomes a mingling of fact with folklore,
but what else, really, is our history?

DEATH IN
EARLY
AMERICA

1

REASONS FOR EARLY DEATH

> I'll pledge my friends,
> And for my foes,
> A plague for their heels
> And a pox for their toes!
> —*A 1651 toast by Dr. William Snelling*

Sickness and death were ubiquitous in earlier times; it is no wonder that Americans who lived before the twentieth century were taught to prepare early for death. On Long Island throughout the seventeenth century young men started in their teens to put away what gold coins they could acquire to pay their funeral expenses. Rural folk especially felt that the seriously ill were "struck with death" and that no one should interfere.

> Friends nor Physicians
> Could not save
> Her marked body
> From the grave.
> —*Early epitaph*

Our ancestors were reconciled to death at any age; that was the will of their Puritan God. A worn monument dated 1818 points out, "The finger of the Lord hath done it."

Families in America during the first three centuries of its existence were many times the size of those today. Parents admitted the obvious: children, frequently the victims of nutritional deficiencies or diarrhea, often did not live beyond infancy. If they survived that, they then ran the gamut of the so-called diseases of childhood—measles, whooping cough, mumps—without the serums that protect today's children. A poignant note in an old history pictures a funeral procession in 1794 near Annville, Pennsylvania, when 150 people on horseback and in carriages followed a young father riding a horse and cradling a small coffin in his arms.

What a melancholy story this epitaph tells:

> Youth behold and shed a tear,
> Fourteen children slumber here.
> See their image how they shine
> Like flowers of a fruitful vine.

Malaria, or "the ague," was so prevalent it was an almost universal complaint, and those suffering from it did not even think of themselves as ill. No one knew then how malaria or yellow fever was carried. Even George Washington, who suffered intermittent attacks of malaria, is supposed to have remarked while reviewing troops in New York State along the southern end of Lake Champlain during the war, "I have never been so much annoyed by mosquitoes in any part of America as in Skenesborough, for that they used to bite through the thickest boot." (Old Skenesborough is today's Whitehall.)

Tuberculosis, also known as "a decline," consumption, and "the great white plague," probably killed more people than any other single disease, and yellow fever was common enough to be known as American distemper. In Philadelphia doctors blamed

This marker mourns the deaths of two children, who died in 1788 and 1789 at the ages of three and four months. Bennington Center Cemetery, Bennington, Vt.

This stone marks the graves of Ann and Mary McKindley, twin sisters. North Cemetery, Galway, N.Y.

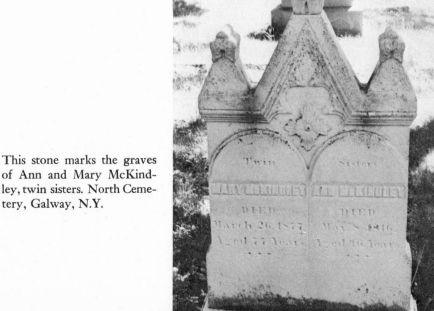

an epidemic on "noxious miasma"—bad air rising from rotting waste or stagnant swamps and the breath of those already infected. People who had to be on the streets held vinegar-soaked handkerchiefs to their noses, wore bags of camphor around their necks, or carried lengths of tarred rope to ward off the disease. Those who could locked themselves indoors and chewed garlic or wore it in their shoes, while they went from room to room whitewashing interior walls. Young fry followed the painters, sprinkling vinegar about and burning gunpowder in each room. At the first suggestion that gunpowder might deter disease, Philadelphians shot at the miasma from the windows of their homes until so many were wounded that the mayor forbade it.

Typhoid fever raged, as we can easily understand, knowing that even the most rudimentary attempts at sanitation were slow to appear. Dysentery, transmitted through uncooked food and drink, was everywhere.

When an epidemic started in a city, families had little effective protection except to move out of the area, a luxury usually permitted only the well-to-do. Excerpts from the daybooks of David Evans, a cabinetmaker in Philadelphia, note:

> Oct. 13, 1793: My family, consisting of myself, my wife and five children, Anne, Sally, Rebecca, John and Eleanor, (my son Evan went there a few weeks before), went to Dr. George DeBenneville's near the city, where we were kindly received and remained three weeks, while the plague raged in the city.

> Nov. 1, 1797: On September 6 I left the city and went to Bristol Township with my family, and returned this evening. Resided at Roberts' school house, while Fever was in the city.

> Sept. 24, 1799: I moved with my family to Eleventh Street between Arch and Race on account of the epidemic Fever, and returned to my house October 19.

Accidents at work and at play used to be common; for example, there were few if any safety regulations in industry and only inadequate inspections of the elements involved in public transportation. Many people were maimed or killed before industry and government set and enforced safety rules. On January 5, 1853, just before Franklin Pierce's inauguration as President of the United States, he, his wife, and their lively thirteen-year-old son were riding the Boston and Maine Railroad from Boston to Concord, New Hampshire, when the axle of a passenger car broke, catapulting cars down an embankment. The boy died, crushed beneath a beam. In 1887 Bussey Bridge near Forest Hills, Massachusetts, collapsed as a train passed over it. Investigators discovered that the company awarded the contract for construction was nonexistent. The company had been merely an idea in the mind of one man, who, alone, had submitted and been awarded the bid, had masterminded and supervised the construction, and received payment. The bridge collapsed because of improperly designed and manufactured iron hangers. No one hired by the railway had inspected the flimsy-looking structure and identified its weakness. Twenty-three people were killed and over a hundred injured when five cars went through the bridge.

Newspapers, letters, and diaries of the centuries preceding this one are filled with calamities that should never have happened, and that never would have happened had modern safety regulations been in effect. Charles Baldwin from Catskill, New York, kept a diary in the 1860's that included a section called "Accidents, Catastrophes, Etc." He listed such items as: explosion of Powder Mills at High Falls; Wesley Sitser severely injured by machinery at Broom Corn Factory; explosion of the boiler on the "Isaac Newton"; Honora Barrigan horribly crushed in machinery in Woolen Mills at Leeds; explosion of locomotive at Catskill Station, fireman died; fall of a span of the old bridge (a fatality occurred here); Abram Leidecker got his foot in the machinery at the Ice-House; a drowning in a bleach-vat at the paper mill; an explosion of the soda-water generator at Smith's Drug Store (three were injured, one fatally). More than one runaway horse was mentioned along with July 4th calamities: "Jed Plimley became sun-struck" and "Melvin Palmer's face was hurt by a rocket."

The decrees of custom also contributed to the number of accidents; as an example, few people knew how to swim.

In colonial days laws approved legal killing in instances that apall us today: a person suspected of arson could be burned at the stake, and some were; couples caught in adultery could be hanged. A population nurtured on Bible reading and the awesome preaching of self-righteous fanatics believed in "an eye for an eye and a tooth for a tooth." Violent crime called out for violent punishment. Capital punishment, frequently in the form of public hangings, brought on a celebration as festive as a fair day, with oysters to eat and "switchel" to drink and peddlers hawking souvenirs.

On June 10, 1809, twenty thousand people gathered in Reading, Pennsylvania, to watch when Susanna Cox was hanged for murdering her infant. Near Norwich, New York, a feud arose between neighbors, Bulldog McCan from Whaupaucau Valley and a farmer named Hatch, when the former's rooster stole grain from Hatch's feed barrel. In a drunken fit, McCan murdered Hatch, and he was tried and sentenced to be hanged. The execution took place in Norwich in front of the courthouse on the day the circus was in town. Its band marched past the gallows as the noose was placed over the culprit's head, and hundreds of eager onlookers heard "They're Hangin' Men an' Women There for Wearin' of the Green," the most appropriate number the musicians knew.

Probably more were killed in our long-drawn-out Indian wars than most people realize. Between 1784 and 1792, for instance, fifteen hundred white settlers were either killed or captured in Kentucky alone.

It has been estimated that twenty thousand men died violent deaths on the Western frontier between 1830 and 1900. Cattle and sheep wars, horse stealing, rustling, dueling over points of honor, and general lawlessness contributed to this total. Notorious gangs roamed the Western states, and one, that of Henry Plummer, was reputed to have killed two hundred men in Idaho and Montana over a short span of years. The Coon Hole Gang in Utah, the Opdyke Gang in Boise City, and lone desperadoes such as Sam Brown, Billy the Kid, Tom Horn, Clay Allison, Wyatt Earp, Boone Helm, and John Slaughter accounted for the deaths of others, the number of which cannot be estimated.

In the South during the 1800's, dueling was at its height, and it was not unusual for individuals with quick tempers and skill with a sword or a pistol to accumulate a dozen or more victims. A seemingly shy, mild-appearing Spaniard from New Orleans, Don José Llulla, know familiarly as Pepe, participated in at least thirty duels, often on behalf of his friends rather than himself. He was a fencing master, expert in the use of the saber, broadsword, and pistol. The author Lafcadio Hearn claims that Pepe's friends were so confident of his ability that they encouraged him to practice by shooting silver dollars from between their thumbs and forefingers. Pepe also owned and operated his own cemetery, the St. Vincent de Paul Cemetery on Louisa Street. There are contradictory reports about whether Pepe encouraged burial of his own victims there.

Statistics on the number killed in duels in the United States would be difficult to obtain, because in time dueling was declared illegal in most states and was usually carried on surreptitiously in the woods outside of town or along the flats by a river or creek.

But the greatest killer in earlier days was not catastrophe, Western violence, dueling, or legal killing, but ignorance. Medical science provided little help in fighting disease until the end of the 1800's. Although the first hospital in this country was opened in Philadelphia in 1752, it was poorly equipped. No anesthesia was used in the United States until 1846, when ether was introduced in Massachusetts General Hospital. Doctors had little knowledge of the need for antiseptics until the end of the 1800's, so until then the septic bacteria, staphylocci and streptococci had a field day.

Poor communication was also a factor. For example, Dr. Ephraim McDowell initiated abdominal surgery by successfully removing an ovarian tumor in 1809. This operation occurred in Danville, on the Kentucky frontier, and it was eight years before it was even reported in a medical journal.

Among the first medical men to arrive in America were Dutchmen, who settled in New Amsterdam (New York City) and along the Hudson River. These men were called *zieckentrooster* or "comforters of the sick." The name was appropriate, for early doctors often did no more than the name implies.

Usually men and women had little faith in the local medical practitioner. Fisher Ames, a congressman who lived in Dedham, Massachusetts, expressed his frustration as a patient: "I am told my case is nervous, bilious, a disease of the liver, atrophy, etc. as different oracles are consulted. I am forbidden and enjoined to take almost everything."

Dan Butts of Tug Hill in northern New York commented:

> Doctors, I suppose they're all right in their way, far as they go, but there ain't one in a thousand that's got the real curing touch, like my old grand-daddy used to have. I remember a salve he used to make out of boneset, spruce pitch, bear's oil, an' a few other things he'd never tell about. Said it would cure any wound or sore that ever was, an' I guess it would. He never went anywhere without a little tin box of it in his pocket, an' it got to be famous all around the country.

Butts goes on to exaggerate the power of Grandpa's salve a mite. He claimed that when his grandpa was soldiering in the Civil War, he was fighting next to a fellow who was decapitated by the thrust of a sharp rebel saber. Gramp applied some of his salve and fastened the head back on. The soldier lived. There was one problem though:

Only thing wrong was that grandpa hurried a little too much an' got the head on backwards. Fellow turned out to be a great scout after that, because the rebels couldn't never tell for sure which way he was looking. . . . But after the war he got to be a terrible thief. Nobody could ever catch him, because they always tracked him the wrong way. Couldn't nobody figure out that he was goin' in the opposite direction from that his tracks p'inted. Things turned out alright, though. After a while they made him sheriff an' he reformed.

In the backcountry herb doctors and "grannies" were often beloved and more popular than the doctor riding the circuit or settling and starting a practice. Aunt Nancy Range was an herb doctor in rural Pennsylvania for fifty years. She rode from patient to patient astride her roan mare, Molly, carrying pills and potions in voluminous saddlebags. She was tall and well-rounded, with a full, high bust, which vibrated as she jogged along. Her eyes were blue-gray, and she tied black strings to her steel-rimmed spectacles so they wouldn't fall off as she rode. When it was cold, she appeared in heavy woolen stockings and a homespun coat trimmed with black braid. Sewn to her long skirts were tremendous pockets, stuffed with treasures, including maple sugar for the children.

Aunt Nancy garnered herbs from the woods: bloodroot, mayapple, sassafras, tag alder, slippery elm, and queen of the meadow, which the Indians used for colds. In her garden she grew foxglove (digitalis comes from this exotic garden plant), catnip, lobelia, peppermint, elecampane, smartweed, goldenseal, spearmint, and spikenard.

This granny possessed a curious mixture of beliefs and became a lay preacher as she got older. Although she had little respect for the Indians who lived near her, she adopted some of their remedies. She was also superstitious, fastening a horseshoe over the door and keeping another in the kitchen to throw into the churn when the butter refused to come. When luck seemed to go against her, she boiled the horseshoe in grease to make everything run smoothly again.

As late as 1837 a cookbook that included some home remedies was published. In it the writer recommended that the doctor should be called only for "inflammation of the bowels," nosebleed, and "gravel" (kidney stones). A home cure for the latter was presented: "Juice of horseradish made into thin syrup mixed with sugar, a spoonful every four hours."

If a city dweller broke a bone, he could be carried to the chirurgeon for the bone to be set. If he was very lucky, the bone knit properly and he was not crippled. Not many sufferers would have been as nonchalant as a gentleman from Brunswick, Maine, named Andrews, whose leg was fractured when a barrel of rum fell on it. While waiting to have his leg set, he blithely composed a poem:

> By a sudden stroke my leg is broke,
>   My heart is sore affended;
> The doctor's come—let's have some rum,
>   And then we'll have it mended.

Playing out-of-doors, children chanted:

> Jack and Jill went up the hill
> To fetch a pail of water.
> Jack fell down and broke his crown,
> And Jill came tumbling after.

> Up Jack got and home did trot
> As fast as he could caper.
> *They put him to bed and plastered his head*
> *With vinegar and brown paper.*

Indoors their parents practiced remedies that sometimes made less sense than those applied to Jack:

For melancholy: Bleed from a vein in the foot.

For goiter: Rub with the hand of a corpse.

For cancer: Anoint affected area several times a day with the juice of the friar's crown (woolly-headed thistle).

For whooping cough: Breathe into your lungs the breath of a fish.

For tapeworms: Take scrapings of pewter spoons, 20–40 grains mixed with sugar.

For a headache: Place a buckwheat cake on the head.

John Ingram, a mustard maker in the Massachusetts Bay Colony, advertised: "It [mustard] is approved by divers eminent Physicians as the only Remedy in the Universe in all Nervous Disorders, sweetens all the Juices, and rectifies the whole Mass of Blood to Admiration."

Dr. John Perkins, practicing in Boston in the early 1700's, prescribed for scrofula (usually tuberculosis affecting the glands) a syrup of sow bugs drowned in white wine, and for palsy a bath in absinthe mixed with "urine hominis," hot.

Urine was used as an ingredient in remedies in other instances. Abraham Wagner, practicing medicine in Pennsylvania in the mid1700's, wrote: "In the neighboring locality of Goschenhoppen a rumor began to float about that a great doctor of medicine had established himself there who wrought miraculous cures . . . from urine."

People swarmed to this doctor from as far as a hundred miles away, and Dr. Wagner again reported, "His medicine caused them to swell up and burst in two, as if they had been poisoned."

If your vision seemed to be failing, Dr. Perkins advised, "Shave your head." Samuel Bent Goldsmith was able to terminate the nocturnal nosebleeds that plagued him by changing his woolen nightcap for a "linnen" one. Dr. Ball of Northboro, Massachusetts Bay Colony, created his own panacea for an itch or, in *his* words, "for the Scratches: One quart fish worms, washed; one pound hog's lard, stewed and filtered; ½ pint of turpentine; ½ pint good brandy. Simmer well and it is fit for use."

DEATH IN EARLY AMERICA

In *Of the Earth Earthy*, Marion Rawson describes the madstone, which existed in the 1800's. Supposedly it drew the poison from a wound, especially after the bite of a mad dog. Both doctors and laymen are said to have sought this rare stone. It was found in the Midwest—light, porous, and green. Legend says it grew in the heart of one buck deer for each deer generation.

Charlotte Scott, whose husband was a doctor, so that we have to believe he approved of this ritual, wrote home from Iowa to her sister in New York State:

> I am surprised to think that you do not use this cold water showering. I know you would not neglect to do so one day if you knew the ease it would give you. Some nights after going to bed my shoulder would pain me so that I could not sleep for hours. I would waken Thomas and go out of doors out of a warm bed, take all my clothes off—he high up on a ladder pouring cold water from the teakettle on my shoulder—so cold that the spatters would freeze in my hair in solid ice. Talk of taking cold—all the injury I received was a good sleep. After the operation the pain was no more for that night.

The mentally ill were subjected to all sorts of indignities, including being imprisoned and chained to walls or being auctioned off to the person in the community who would keep them for the least money. Court records in Philadelphia explain that in 1678 Jan Cornelissen

> complains to the court that his son Erick is bereft of his natural senses, and is turned quite mad, and he, not being able to maintain him, it was ordered that three or four persons be hired to build a little block house, and there to confine him—expenses to be provided for in the next levy or tax.

The Hartford (Connecticut) Retreat, which opened in 1824, and the first state asylum (Worcester, Massachusetts), which opened in 1833, were pioneer institutions; however, anyone who happened to be different was apt to be isolated as if he were unclean or possessed of evil spirits.

Also, in Pennsylvania, the powwowing of "witch doctors" was known. This ritual incorporated a faith in magical powers. If, for example, a witch doctor wished to remove a goiter, a ceremony would be performed as the moon waxed. He would pass his hand over the growth, repeating, "What I see must increase, what I feel must decrease. What I see must increase, what I feel must decrease."

It was believed in Bedford County, Pennsylvania, that if a person suffered a severe wound, the bleeding might be stopped by reciting from the Bible:

> And when I passed by thee, and saw thee polluted in thine own blood, I said unto thee when thou wast in thy blood, Live; yea, I said unto thee, when thou wast in thy blood, Live.
> —Ezekiel, 16:6–7

The author of *Reminiscences and Sketches* says:

> I have conversed with intelligent men of age and experience, and in numbers not a few, who are firm believers in this, and who say they must believe it for they have seen it done. And they relate instances of divers kind where, as they think, people would have bled to death but for the use of this mystic verse. And it is not necessary that the faith-operator shall be present with the person or animal who is bleeding. They tell how a messenger had gone in hot haste and how, as was verified afterward by a comparison of time, the blood ceased to flow at the very minute the verse was repeated.

From the manuscript of Dr. Zerobabel Endecott of Salem, Massachusetts, comes this prescription for a woman having a difficult time in childbirth: "Take a lock of hair from a virgin who is exactly one-half the age of the patient; pulverize this. Take one dozen ant eggs which have been dried in an oven. Mix the first two ingredients with ¼ pint of milk from a red cow and dose the patient."

Theo, the young son of Charles Baldwin, the stonecutter and diarist, had what his doctor called "cerebro-spinal-meningitis" and suffered from intermittent convulsions for days. Dr. Mackay prescribed alternate applications of bruised horseradish leaves and pepper sauce applied to the back until it was almost blistered, and bruised plantain leaves. Inexplicably, the infant recovered. Doctors of the day believed that raising blisters on the skin by use of a counterirritant would bring an internal inflammation to the outside of the body. Such practices often caused severe burns and excruciating pain.

The custom of bleeding patients was brought here by European colonists and practiced for over two centuries. Dr. Samuel Fuller, who arrived on the *Mayflower*, wrote of going from Plymouth to Matapan (now Dorchester) to visit patients requiring medical service there. He mentioned that he "let some 20 people's blood" and "had conference with them till I was weary." Joseph Denison, a tutor at Yale, complained that during an illness he was drained of about a gallon of blood—"blooded once or twice a day"— during a ten-day illness. Perhaps he was bled into a pewter porringer; these have been referred to as "bleeding cups."

If Joseph lost only a gallon of blood, he was lucky; it has been estimated that the average bloodletting took a pint of blood. Doctors in earlier times believed, incorrectly, of course, that a gland within the body replaced blood and that the replacement took place within hours rather than the weeks it actually takes. Doctors' ledgers and medical books show that the ill were bled for an unbelievable variety of complaints: gastritis, enteritis, colic, inflammation of the bladder and the liver, inflammation of the eyes, of the lungs, and of the throat—for the latter, bleeding from the jugular vein was recommended—kidney stones, hemorrhoids, earache, jaundice, gout, varicose veins, dog bite, epilepsy, palsy, apoplexy, intermittent fevers, remittent fevers, pulmonary consumption, smallpox, measles, asthma.

Early in our history there were quacks as well as those who compounded potions in good faith. In Smartville, New York, Henry Schermerhorn operated a pill factory in the 1800's. His chief ingredients were herb extracts and flour dough. The pills were rolled by hand, dried, and coated with sugar. Mr. "Scammyhorn's" pills were supposed to be laxative, but neighbors who saw a rooster gobble up a whole batch that had been placed in the sun to dry could see little effect on the rooster for better or for worse. Henry also marketed a salve made in semisolid sticks about three inches long and an inch in diameter. These sticks were wrapped in heavy oiled paper and had to be held over a candle or match flame to be softened for use. The manufacturer's younger brother, Abe, distributed the remedies by horse and wagon.

Around the beginning of the nineteenth century, a pioneer family was crossing Pennsylvania when the father was taken ill and died. The only medical practitioner available, a man named Miller, who also took care of the animal population in the community, was called in. He diagnosed the malady of the deceased as yellow fever and prescribed his powders, at fifty cents a dose, for the rest of the family. Despite the precautionary measures, other members of the family sickened, and a son died. Dr. Marchand from Greensburg was sent for this time. He discovered that the father had died of a stroke, and that other members of the family were suffering from malaria contracted from exposure on their difficult journey. Analysis of the prescribed powders proved that they had been concocted largely from brick dust.

For years after America was colonized, and even after the Revolutionary War, most women in labor were attended by midwives rather than by male doctors. This was almost exclusively true before 1750. In rural areas midwives continued to assist in childbirth well into the twentieth century, and in the backcountry of the South there are still a few to be found. Modern midwives have often been trained by teams from public health agencies. Colonial communities accepted varying degrees of responsibility to encourage these women. New Amsterdam officials provided a home for their resident midwife, Lysbert Dircken. Later records show the payment of one hundred guilders annually to Hellezond Jaris for taking over the same office. A tombstone in a Charleston, South Carolina, cemetery records that Mrs. Eliza Phillips of that city assisted in the birth of three thousand infants, while a remarkable Lydia Robinson of New London, Connecticut, boasted—as well she might—of delivering twelve hundred babies over a thirty-five-year span *without losing one.*

Among early midwives there were apt to be superstitious practices. Many believed:

1. If a patient hemorrhaged, an ax placed blade side up under the bed would stop the bleeding.
2. A knife under a pillow would help cut pain.
3. A mother's milk could be encouraged to dry up if she expressed some upon a hot rock.
4. A pan of water under the bed would help to lower the patient's temperature.

Some of the earliest male doctors represented themselves as "male midwives." This was true of Dr. James Floyd, who studied in London, then returned to his native Boston during the late eighteenth century.

Today preventive medicine saves thousands of lives a year. When, in 1721, Cotton Mather, Dr. Zabdiel Boylston, and a few cohorts recommended inoculation for smallpox during an epidemic, most people thought they were insane. Inoculation became the most controversial topic of the day. Later, vaccination was introduced, employing serum derived from cows. The enemies of vaccination pictured men and women sprouting horns and mooing. Believers were as vocal in their efforts to encourage inoculation. When Samuel Ward, Governor of Rhode Island and a member of the Continental Congress, died in 1776, of smallpox, John Adams sputtered:

> We have this week lost a very valuable friend of the colonies in Governor Ward of Rhode Island, by the smallpox in the natural way. He never would harken to his friends who have constantly been advising him to be inoculated ever since the first Congress began. But he would not be persuaded. Numbers, who have been inoculated, have gone through this distemper without any danger, or even confinement. But nothing would do; he must take it in the natural way and die.

There was, though, reason to be wary. Some died from complications that arose after inoculation. Jonathan Edwards, the preacher-evangelist who was president of Princeton, (then the College of New Jersey) was one of these. When he took office as president of the college in February 1758, there were cases of smallpox in Princeton. His doctor and his closest friends persuaded Edwards that he and other members of the family should be inoculated. A physician from Philadelphia was summoned, and on February 23 the inoculation was performed. On March 22 Edwards died. His daughter, Mrs. Burr (mother of Aaron), had been inoculated along with her father. She seemed to recover, but sixteen days after her father's death, she, too, was dead. A doctor diagnosed the cause of her demise: "a messenger was sent suddenly to call her out of the world."

An epitaph from a grave marker in a Vernon, Vermont, cemetery comments further:

> Here lies cut down, like unripe fruit,
> A son of Mr. Amos Tute . . .
> To death he fell a helpless prey,
> On April 5 and Twentieth Day,
> In seventeen hundred seventy-seven,

Quitting this world, we hope, for Heaven . . .
Behold the amazing alteration,
Effected by inoculation;
The means employed his life to save,
Hurried him headlong to the grave.

In the late 1700's and during the 1800's, families sometimes joined together for inoculations and the resulting confinements. An appropriate home would be chosen; folks would be inoculated and then stay together for the duration of their induced illnesses. In *We Were New England*, S. G. Goodrich of Ridgefield, Connecticut, describes such a cooperative hospitalization in the home of a friend. Provisions were ordered and delivered to an agreed-upon spot "down the lane" for pickup by one of the patients.

In 1805 the account book of Dr. Joshua Webster records charges of eight shillings, or about two dollars, for vaccination. A man who called himself Dr. Sylvanus Fancher specialized in vaccinating. He had invented an instrument for making the incision—a silver bar with a concealed lancet—which he claimed was highly efficient. Fancher was an itinerant, and traveled widely, offering his services. He is described as wearing "velvet small-clothes, a parti-colored waistcoat from which dangled a half a dozen watch-chains and trinkets for the amusement of the little folks, and a faded blue coat—all of these surmounted by a slouched hat overhanging green goggles."

It is hardly fair to satirize cures suggested by early medical men without at least reminding readers how physicians learned their trade. Most of our first doctors learned as apprentices over a period of from three to five years. Usually they lived with their mentors, helping with household and farm chores to defray the additional costs in firewood, food, and lights, which their presence occasioned. For the doctor, they fed, held, curried, and drove the horses, swept the office, answered the door, and scoured instruments and bottles. After a while the students were allowed to grind powders and pills. Later they assisted in bleeding patients and applying poultices. The older physicans taught their apprentices to keep casebooks and allowed them to read their manuals.

There *were* medical schools. The first, at the College of Philadelphia, opened in 1765. Yale and Harvard, Berkshire Medical Institution in Massachusetts, and Castleton Medical College in Vermont were popular. Transylvania in Lexington, Kentucky, was the medical center of the West. Jefferson Medical College in Philadelphia, Ohio College, Louisville Medical Institute, and Massachusetts General in Boston competed for illustrious faculty and eager medical students. The apprenticeship system, though, remained important well into the nineteenth century. For example, Dr. Joshua Webster's ledger records that "Martin Boofie commenced the Study of Physick with me on this day Aug. 2, 1803."

In the cities respected doctors sometimes gave a series of lectures to benefit their less-experienced colleagues. In Philadelphia in 1762 Dr. William Shippen and Dr. John Morgan planned a course on "anatomy and midwifery accompanied by dissections." *The Pennsylvania Gazette* of November 15, 1762, advised:

> Dr. Shippen's Anatomy Lectures will begin tomorrow evening at six o'clock, in his father's house, in Fourth Street. Tickets for the Course may be had of the Doctor at five Pistoles each and any gentlemen who incline to see the subject prepared for the lecture and learn the art of Dissecting, Injections, etc. are to pay five Pistoles more.

David Evans (the Philadelphia cabinetmaker mentioned before) noted in his daybook: "Nov. 9, 1799—Dr. Benjamin Rush, to making 1 Mahogany Bureau Table 4/7/10, as a compensation for my son Evan Evans' ticket of admission attending his Lectures for 1798."

Old-time doctors were apt to be part-timers, and this was a disadvantage. The first Dutch *zieckentrooster* was a schoolmaster.

In New Amsterdam Dr. Abram Staats was a medical man and a fur trader. Businessmen sometimes took up medicine because it was prestigious socially. In old Connecticut Dr. Jasper Gunn was a doctor, a tinker, and a surveyor. Griffith Owen, who journeyed to Philadelphia with William Penn, was a minister and a physician. Dr. Scott, who practiced medicine in Iowa in the mid-1800's, was also a farmer and a postmaster.

False modesty was another handicap to doctors. An old print shows one taking a woman's pulse with just her hand extended from a heavily curtained bedstead. In Pennsylvania in communities of the "plain folk," doctors often used to deliver babies by touch. The patients were completely covered by sheets!

Another story illustrates a lady's modesty. In the early 1800's a pair of elderly sisters and a courtly gentleman, who happened to be the town doctor, dined together each week. This was the day of the tall porcelain chamber pail, and one of the sisters, both of whom were rather plump, accidentally cracked and broke this bedroom necessity, falling heavily upon the splintered china. The doctor was summoned by a maid. Upon arrival he saw only one sister, in bed, thoroughly muffled except for the injured part of her anatomy. Without identifying his patient, the doctor carefully removed the china and gently applied antiseptics. When he called the following week, *both* sisters were seated upon soft cushions.

Doctors were poorly paid and only infrequently received cash. In 1755 Dr. Cornelius Van Dyck of Schenectady, New York, received among other items, tea, rum, sugar, and a cowhide. In Albany one doctor encouraged yearly contracts; he exchanged his services to one patient for ten beaver skins.

Dr. Samuel Loomis, according to ledger entries in 1784, received among his payments five thousand shingles, six framed chairs, window sashes, and a large iron kettle. In 1789 Dr. John Watrous was given a load of clover hay, a fourth of a lamb, four barrels, and several payments through services. One debt was canceled by "digging beets for ½ day," another for "3 days of digging stone," another after a day's work "shoveling dung." In 1825 payments were made to a doctor in furniture, one old cutter, a sixth of a ticket in the Washington Canal Lottery of August 13, and storage of the doctor's furniture for a period of time. For inoculating Captain Benjamin Hine's children in Waterbury, Connecticut, Dr. Abel Bronson received homespun.

Before 1782 in Boston—cash was more plentiful in the cities— patients usually paid from one shilling, six pence to two shillings per daytime call. Night calls cost double this amount.

The account books of several doctors are enlightening. That of Dr. Van Dyck of Schenectady for the years 1754 and 1755 lists the names of his patients, his services to them, and the charges:

Henrick Veeder—To a strengthening plaister	0/1/6
Debora Wing—viol of eye water	0/2/0
Pieter Ouderkerk—To a purge for the wench	0/2/0
to bleeding	0/1/6
to 20 doses of pills	0/10/0
to cordial drops	0/8/0
to purging portion for the year	0/2/6
Jan Babbitt Wendall	
to bleeding	0/1/6
to a vomit dose	0/2/0
to 10 powders	0/5/0
to powder to stop bleeding	0/0/6
to a mixture for the feavor	0/4/0
to drawing your tooth	0/2/0
to purging potion	0/2/0

The names of Harmanus Brat, Abraham Vredenborg, Jacob Hunstrat, John Vrooman, and Symon Scharhorn were among those listed with the notation "Serving your wife."

The medical account book of Dr. John Watrous of Colchester, Connecticut, covers the time from 1781 to 1798. A few items follow:

Dorus, a Negro—rectify his wrist   0/1/6
Cesar, a Negro—Credit—by working mortar   0/0/9
                 cutting 3 loads of wood 0/8/0

The methods by which Dr. Watrous was paid are varied, as was the custom. Ichabod Buel received a credit of 0/7/2 for 165 floor spikes; Enos Williams, a credit of 1/2/6 for quantities of corn and cheese; Samuel Freeman paid with three casks of wheat; Esther Blish worked off her debt by spinning linen yarn for 1/7/6 and hetcheling flax for 1/0/0.

By 1826 Dr. Robert Frary of Hudson, New York, was keeping his accounts in dollars and cents:

William Free—pulled tooth	.25
John Dayton—bleeding and cathartic	1.00
Nicholas Hughson's wife—obstetric attendance	5.00
Leonard Winston—blue pills	
County of Columbia—female prisoner venereal attendance	5.00
Theophilus Ransom—for Self, venereal medicine and advice	5.00
Moses Derby—cathartic yesterday	.62½
cream of tartar this day	.62½

Jay Barnes, a peddler who lived at the foot of Wheat Hill, east of Lacona, New York, later in the 1800's promised to pay his doctor's bill with a load of hay, but he neglected to deliver. Meeting and stopping to pass the time of day, the two conversed:

Doc (sarcastically): Say, Jay, that certainly was a dandy load of hay you brought me.
Jay (genially): Well now, Doc, I'm sure glad you liked it. I feel the same way about your doctorin'. Tell you what I'm goin' to do. I'm gonna bring you another load out of the same mow, and it won't cost you a cent!

About 1810 the Clinton County Medical Society in upper New York State agreed upon these charges:

Fee for each visit .25
Riding per mile .20
Doctor in night .38
Consultation 1.00
Cathartics .13–.25

And in the 1830's, it has been estimated, successful rural doctors received about five hundred dollars a year in cash and barter.

One of the earliest American medical treatises to be published was *A Brief Guide to the Small-Pox and Measles,* written by the Reverend Thomas Thatcher in 1677 and published in the scientifically oriented city of Philadelphia. Dr. William Buchan, an Englishman, later published a medical manual which proved especially popular. An American edition was printed in 1848. This was called *Domestic Medicine or A Treatise on the Prevention and Cure of Diseases by Regimen and Simple Medicines: With Observations on Sea-Bathing, and the Use of the Mineral Waters, to Which Is Annexed a Dispensatory for the Use of Private Practitioners.* Buchan suggested bleeding as a treatment for almost every malady he listed. A few of his statements and prescriptions make sense today; many do not.

He comments, "Almost one-half of the human species perish in infancy, by improper management or neglect." He warns:

> Studious persons are very subject to the gout. This painful disease in a great measure proceeds from indigestion and an obstructed perspiration. . . . The studious are likewise very liable to the stone and gravel. . . . No person ought either to take violent exercise, or to study immediately after a full meal. . . . In the above remarks on the usual diseases of the studious, my chief object was to warn them of the evil consequences of *painful* and *intense* thinking.

Buchan discusses some of the causes of illness:

> . . . beds become damp, either from their not being used, standing in damp houses, or in rooms without

fire, or from the linen not being dry when laid on the bed. Nothing is to be more dreaded by travellers than damp beds, which are very common in all places where fuel is scarce. . . . Beds kept in private families for the reception of strangers are often equally dangerous. . . . All the bad occurrences from this quarter might easily be prevented in private families, by causing their servants to sleep in the spare beds and resign them to strangers when they come. . . . That baneful custom said to be the practice in many inns, of damping sheets and pressing them, in order to save washing, and afterwards laying them on the beds, ought, when discovered, to be punished with the utmost severity. It is really a species of murder, and will often prove as fatal as poison or gunshot.

Rooms are often rendered damp by an unseasonable piece of cleanliness; I mean the pernicious custom of washing them immediately before company is put into them. Most people catch cold if they sit but a very short time in a room that has been lately washed.

Buchan comments on the methods used to cool off in warm weather, saying that to sit by an open window is "a dangerous custom." He is especially vehement when he suggests that all beware of plunging themselves, when hot, into cold water. This may cause fever, but worse yet, "madness, itself, has frequently been the effect of this conduct."

Should a patient have a fever, he should drink tea made from the following, which he might "bruise together":

> 1 ounce of gentian root
> ½ ounce of calamus aromaticus
> ½ ounce of orange peel
> 3 or 4 handfuls of camomile flowers
> a handful of coriander seeds

The doctor belittles the use of spiders, cobwebs, and snuffings from candles in case of fever, although he admits that they may sometimes succeed.

"Peruvian bark" (quinine) is prescribed appropriately at times. Dr. Buchan says, "Children have been cured of agues by making them wear a waistcoat with powdered bark quilted between the folds of it." Mercury, used to combat syphilis, was another early medication that worked.

According to Buchan,

> Miliary fever is sometimes occasioned by violent passions or affectations of the mind; as excessive grief, anxiety, thoughtfulness, etc. This fever takes its name from the small pustules or bladders which appear on the skin, resembling in shape and size the seeds of the millet. . . . This disease in childbed women is sometimes the effect of great costiveness during pregnancy; it may likewise be occasioned by their excessive use of green trash [leafy vegetables?] and other unwholesome things which pregnant women are apt to indulge.

For hemorrhaging the medic advised "old conserve of red roses mixed with new, mild conserve—one ounce given 3 or 4 times daily." To be more specific, for a nosebleed, Buchan would have his patient sit upright with his head reclining a little and his legs immersed in water the temperature of new milk. His garters should be tightened. Another nosebleed remedy was to immerse the head in a pail of cold water containing muriate of ammonia and common salt. If the patient preferred, he could snuff vinegar in cold water up his nose. And, for a sure cure, Dr. Buchan advised, "If the genitals be immersed in cold water for some time, it will generally stop a bleeding at the nose."

Many old-time medical practitioners performed services reserved today for dentists or veterinarians. An entry in a nineteenth-century doctor's ledger includes an item "for castrating a horse." Few early dentists worked at that livelihood all of the time. Often barbers acted as dentists. Along with barber-dentists, there was at least one jeweler-dentist, Dr. Richard Griswold of Bainbridge, New York, familiarly know as Little Dick.

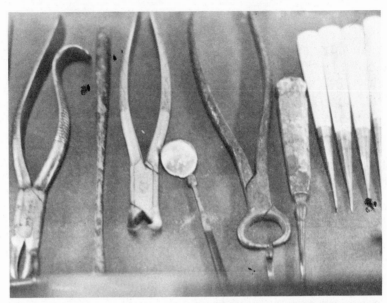

Old dentist's tools.   *Courtesy Old Fort Museum, Schoharie, N.Y.*

Others practicing part-time dentistry were tinkers, metalworkers, or clock menders as well. Known to be active in 1822 was a specialist in dentistry named Brockway, who traveled a north-south route, usually in Vermont, between Albany and Canada. Perhaps it was Brockway about whom Nathaniel Hawthorne reported in 1838 in his ever-present notebook:

> A young fellow, twenty or thereabouts pained with a toothache. A doctor, passing on horseback, with his black leather saddlebags behind him, a thin frosty-haired man. Being asked to operate, he looks at the tooth, lances the gum, and the fellow being content to be dealt with on the spot, he seats himself in a chair on the stoup with great heroism. The doc produces a rusty pair of iron forceps, a man holds the patient's head. . . . A turn of the doctor's hand, and the tooth is out. The patient gets up, half-amazed, pays the doc ninepence, pockets the tooth, and the spectators are in glee and admiration.

Another time Hawthorne mentions a traveling surgeon-dentist who

> has taken a room in the North Adams House and sticks up his advertising bills on the pillars of the piazza & all about town. He is a tall, slim young man, dressed in a country-made coat of light blue (taken as he tells me, in exchange for dental operations), black pantaloons, and clumsy, cowhide boots. . . . He is not only a dentist, which trade he follows temporarily, but a licensed preacher of the Baptist persuasion.

Wood and ivory from the hippopotamus were used to manufacture false teeth; gold was used for fillings. If it was necessary to extract several teeth on the same side of the mouth, the dentist provided "plumpers" which the patient could insert to keep his cheeks from looking hollow. There are portraits of George Washington with and without his plumpers. The Stuart portrait seems to show him "with." Washington owned two sets of dentures when the well-known portrait was painted; both were noisy and ill-fitting.

Among the most famous practitioners of early American dentistry was Paul Revere, who advertised that he had fixed hundreds of teeth and was prepared to attend any gentleman or lady at his or her own home. The services of dentists were accepted when offered, although this happened in cities more often than in the country. The enlightened attempted to keep their teeth clean by scouring with a cherry twig, and old wives continued to suggest, "If your tooth aches, pick it with a coffin nail or a needle which has been used to sew a shroud."

Dr. Buchan noted:

> Some pretend to have found great benefit in the tooth-ache, from the application of an artificial magnet to the affected tooth. . . . Keeping the teeth clean has, no doubt, a tendency to prevent the tooth-ache. The

best method of doing this is to wash them daily with salt and water, a decoction of the bark, or with cold water alone. All brushing and scraping of the teeth is dangerous.

Another doctor suggested that teeth be cleaned with a preparation of prepared oyster shell, chalk made from mussels, seasoning, and flavoring.

Many early doctors were selfless, completely sincere and altruistic people who just didn't possess the knowledge necessary to effect cures. The accurate diagnosis of ills was infrequent and often impossible. Many must have been terribly frustrated. Dr. Peter Bryant, father of the better-known poet-editor William Cullen Bryant, started his practice in 1792 in Cummington, Massachusetts, after an apprenticeship under his father in Bridgewater, Connecticut. In his words, ". . . with my small stock of book knowledge, without experience in the ways of the world, my whole property consisting of a horse, a few books, about $25 worth of medicine, I launched out into the world to begin business." Twenty-one years later he was still concerned about his inadequacies and worrying about the death of a patient. "I have been wholly unable to satisfy myself as to the cause of his death. It could not have been *apoplexy* . . . it could not be *convulsion*, for there was no contortion of limbs and countenance." Then Bryant falls back on the justification for death that is so evident among the epitaphs of olden times. "It was the divine will; and may God of His infinite mercy make it a profitable lesson to us."

From another doctor's diary: "Widow Alcock died of a hot bread supper." "Justice Billings did so of eating Brown Bread for breakfast, a Thing he never used before."

Medical men tormented themselves with questionings. If a patient died, they tried to learn from the evidence that was obvious to them. When a patient lived after following their advice, they were not sure whether or not the advice had helped.

REASONS FOR EARLY DEATH

In central New York in the early 1800's, a lumberman of Norwich, Whitman Wilcox, took logs by raft down the Susquehanna each spring. One year a Mr. Rathburn, an acquaintance who was ill, asked if he might make the trip downstream with the lumberman. His doctor had suggested that if Mr. Rathburn could get to the ocean he might improve. Wilcox hesitated, volunteering the opinion that raft fare of corn cakes and beans wasn't intended for invalids. He thought, too, that Rathburn's condition might worsen from exposure to the weather. Mr. Rathburn, who suspected that his doctor's advice had been a last resort, convinced Wilcox that he wanted to risk the trip. The two traveled down the Susquehanna and back; the sick man recovered completely and lived for years, advising all and sundry who were ill to travel to the seacoast. Certainly, though, the doctor never knew exactly what caused the patient's recovery.

The diary of S. R. Rockwell, M.D., of East Windsor Hill, in South Windsor, Connecticut, provides further insight into a doctor's dilemma.

> Rode all day visiting patients. Have two or three that trouble me much.
> Poor old Mrs. Watson has been in a fit all day and is still speechless at one A.M.
> The child with croup is apparently no worse. I hope it will recover.
> I was out last P.M. attending Mrs. Calvin Parsons who gave birth to a female child, the fourth living one.
> I attended on a jury . . . the wife of Sampson Dunn who was driven from the house and froze to death.
> Peace reigns in the Insane Department and people generally better nurtured throughout the House.
> Mrs. Perrine quite sick and at present quite difficult to tell what ails her, a singular fever.
> Poor Miss Kempton is very poorly and I fear will be obliged to leave us.

Thus many who today would need only a dose of a new drug

or a few days' treatment in a hospital were, despite the efforts of their doctors, "obliged to leave."

Some statistics on life expectancy were compiled by Dr. Edward A. Holyoke of Salem, Massachusetts, and reported in 1789: Sixty-two towns in Massachusetts and New Hampshire were used to gather the figures. At that time a woman might expect to live until she was 36.5; a man could look forward to 34.5 years of life. If a person survived infancy, though, according to Holyoke, he was apt to live to be fifty or sixty. He, himself, lived to be a hundred!

Statistics were also gathered among the Shakers of the Enfield Colony. They were based on a small sampling, but the first figure, at least, bears out Dr. Holyoke's research. Between 1793 and 1800 the average age at death was 34.7. However, life expectancy improved at a faster rate among the Shakers than it did in the outside world. Again from their figures we find that life expectancy between 1821 and 1830 was 50.7; between 1851 and 1860, 54.9; and between 1881 and 1890, 66.9.

The Shakers estimated that in the nineteenth century death among their members was delayed a decade. They laid this to their "sexual purity." There were probably many factors, including regular daily routine, a wholesome diet, excellent care for the aged, and freedom from worry about providing life's necessities. Are you familiar with adult-sized invalid cradles? These were used by the Shakers, who gently rocked their aged ill and senile from this world into another.

Insurance companies today tell us that we should expect to live to be over seventy.

2

BIOGRAPHICAL SKETCH

OF A NINETEENTH-CENTURY DOCTOR: EX-
CERPTS FROM LETTERS BETWEEN MEMBERS
OF THE FAMILY OF DR. THOMAS SCOTT,
1847–1865.

"If the Devil was sick and sent for him
he would surely go."
—From a letter written by a doctor's wife.

In the late 1840's Charlotte Wray, who lived with her family
near Granville, New York, met and gave in to the entreaties of
Thomas Scott, who begged her to marry him and go west to
Iowa, where he intended to set up a medical practice. His family
home had been on Isle La Motte, one of the beautiful Vermont
islands at the northern end of Lake Champlain; already his parents
had left there to travel west and settle in Iowa.

The Thomas Scotts journeyed west in 1847 and, after living

for six months with Thomas's cousin, moved into their own home, which Thomas had built in an area called Garnaville. (Although I have found no reference to this, it seems to me that the Scotts must have selected the name, transposing and adding letters until Granville became Garnaville.)

Thomas started his practice, evidently riding a circuit as judges, preachers, and doctors of that era often did. He bought additional lands, built first a log cabin and then a larger home in nearby Farmersburgh, where he also operated a farm. By 1853 the Scotts were living in Monona, a short distance from their first homes. Charlotte bore three children: Winfield, who died at seven, Mary Elvira, who survived for only a few hours, and Cora.

Thomas orated at temperance meetings, was appointed post-master of Monona, managed his farm, was superintendent of Sabbath day school, and led an altogether busy life. Ironically, in the brief span of fifteen years, this young man, who practiced medicine as seriously and sincerely as he knew how, lost all except one of those who were closest to him—and each was his patient—his son Winfield; his infant daughter; his mother; his youngest brother, twenty-year-old Henry; and finally, in 1863, his wife Charlotte.

The quotations I have chosen give the flavor of the life of one country doctor in the Midwest in the middle of the nineteenth century. The excerpts are from letters that have been saved in my family. Most were written by Charlotte to her sister, Martha Wray Madison, back in Granville. A few notes were written by Thomas.

Garnaville, September 12, 1847, Thomas to Father Wray:

> Charlotte tells me you supposed she would help me fix my drugs. Well indeed she makes the old iron mortar rattle well when I am in a hurry. Every viol must be corked just so tightly, and every paper in just such style and she seems to take as much delight in

aiding me to compound my medicines as I do in having her by me when at my books.

Garnaville, November 4, 1847, Charlotte to Martha:

Thomas is gone now. He went away Monday and I do not expect him home until Saturday night. His ride extends a great distance—to Alcador, Turkey River and down to Delaware County. But I care not as long as he is making money. So much for having a doctor for a husband.

. . . I often look at the last work Mother done for me, that coverlet I hold as sacred, that little brass kettle she last presented to me. . . . I have been studying medicine books, principles of midwifery. I am getting a good knowledge of that I think. Perhaps I shall go with Thomas to all such places. I have been twice. What think you of that?

Garnaville, April 23, 1848, Charlotte to Martha [Thomas's mother is ill.]:

. . . I think the slender thread will soon be broken that keeps her from the sainted dead. She is perfectly resigned. She waits God's appointed time with great patience. How easy is the death bed of the righteous.

Garnaville, July 2, 1848, Charlotte to Martha:

Look into Scott's east room, his study, and there you will see Charlotte writing or trying to write. She looks about the same as when you last saw her. The room is carpeted with the prettiest carpet in Iowa, the same one that was woven by Sis. We have a new set of chairs and sofa, a toilet table and looking glass and the library looks very nice. Don't you think our room is pleasant? There is more in the room. I have two bowls of plants, wild rose and portulaces. They are in blossom. Come stay longer. I am alone again. Thomas will be from home till tomorrow night. . . .

11 o'clock. Thomas came home tired and sleepy but don't stop to rest he is teacher in sabbath school hurries

there hears his class recite and then was called another
way. That's the way he performs. He is not idle one
moment. He is bound to have riches and honor and
there is no doubt but he will accomplish his design. . . .

The fourth is near at hand . . . we did intend going
to Prairie LaPort, a town on the Mississippi. They
intend giving a dinner, having an oration (Subject
Indian Mounds) and having a ball in the evening. But
Thomas was obliged to stay at home on some woman's
account—case of midwifery. . . . I had a present of a
new dress and a whole piece of cotton. What a good
Thomas! I think that all the time.

Garnaville, August 8, 1848, Charlotte to Martha:

Thomas is from home a great part of the time. No: I
will not be lonely for his business calls him from home
and when I am alone here in my chamber I have this
dear dear miniature to look at and plenty of good
books to read. . . . This region of light and darkness is
infested with large rattlesnakes, small wolves, cata-
mounts, and Prairie bachelors, so when I go out I
have to keep my big eyes open. . . .

My pen is like a duck's foot—I have to scratch twice
to make a letter and my candle is made of lard, the
wick a rag and candlestick a saucer. . . .

Pa Scott's family enjoy poor health. Ma has had
erysypilus six months or more and no use of one hand
and is quite lame also. Henry has the ague. And Betsey
is out of health. I brought her home with me. I think
I can cure her.

Garnaville, August 13, 1848, Thomas to Father Wray:

. . . I presume you would like to know what I have
been doing since I came to Iowa. Well, I will tell you.
When I came hither I was in debt to my brother and
father and I was then without bridle, horse or saddle.
I now have to pay my brother $100; when which is
paid I shall be out of debt. I can take $250 for my
house in town any day. My horse and saddle are worth

$75. I have a cookstove for which I paid $27 and also a good new set of dining chairs and accounts outstanding for which I would not take less than $150. So you have my stewardship for last year.

Garnaville, October 10, 1848, Charlotte to Martha:

You may like to know what and how we are doing. Well, 'tis a horrid healthy time now, nobody sick. Thomas has sold his house and lots for a house and 40 acres of land some eight miles from here "out in the country" as they say. This land is under good improvements and joins the land he has so he will have a good farm and if he has no practice there will be something coming in.

Garnaville, April 1849, Charlotte to Martha:

My time has been devoted to reading the work of Dr. Fitch "Of consumption cured" a grand work. I wish you could read it. He recommends bathing in cold water daily. We have adopted that practice. He also recommends shoulder braces for all persons consumptive or those who have a disposition to stooping. I wear the braces.

Farmersburgh, September 1849, Charlotte to Martha:

My head aches and I feel somewhat depressed. I had my teeth cleaned and filled yesterday so that may be the cause of it. Thomas' uncle, Mr. Derby, from Wisconsin was here on a visit and being a dentist done a good job for us—repaired our corngrinders. We have had a sick man here to be doctored up, difficulty in his chest. He is now well. He is to work for us now for a while in harvest. Grain is now ripe for the sickle.

Farmersburgh, December 21, 1849, Charlotte to Martha [Martha has complained of a sore shoulder.]:

You know my shoulder has pained me much for two years past and I am now trying something which I think is far superior to Dr. Scott's or Dr. Fitch's braces. Tis simply the pure cold water. Bare your shoulder or strip all off, no matter. Then go down cellar and let me stand high on the stairs and pour it out of the teakettle slowly upon your spine from your neck down, no matter how cold. If ice 'tis better. Two kettles full is best. Makes you shiver a little at first but what of that? I like it well now, don't even quiver. I rest well at night. Give it a try.

Farmersburgh, March 29, 1850, Charlotte to Martha:

. . . We are in trouble now. For death is not long in selecting its victims. Thomas' brother was buried yesterday, a young man in the prime of life, promising much comfort to his aging parents. But alas he was taken away suddenly in three short days from health to the grave. He was the last child that was left at home. Now they, father and mother, are left alone. The blow was a hard one but they bore it well. He died with the brain fever. I never knew of a death that affected me more. But poor fellow is sleeping his last sleep and his remains are interred in sight of our house.

Farmersburgh, June 16, 1850, Charlotte to Martha:

You well know when we came here we had nothing. Thomas in debt to his father for his medicines which he bought there and our expense money getting here. Thomas has been disappointed for it is not as good a place as he had expected for his profession. It is too healthy here for a man to get rich very soon by dosing the sick.

Farmersburgh, June 26, 1851, Charlotte to Martha:

Thomas has gone to see Betsey his youngest sister. She has a young child one week old and has a broken breast—been lanced 7 times and has broken 8. She is very low. We think her recovery doubtful. [Betsey lived and later went with her husband and children to California.]

BIOGRAPHICAL SKETCH

Farmersburgh, July 19, 1851, Charlotte to Martha:

Thomas was called away yesterday in the upper country. Came home today. Bought him a new horse for $85. Staid at home about 5 minutes and put out again so you can see I am left a widow quite often.

Monona, February 14, 1853, Thomas to Martha and James:

I have been reading, filling a tooth for Charlotte, cracking some hickory nuts and gabbing lots with my wife.

Monona, May 1, 1853, Charlotte to Martha [Thomas appointed postmaster]:

So I shall have something to do. Besides being confined at home—that will be hard for me for Thomas has bought a new buggy and I was making great reckoning of riding around the country with him this summer, but I have been out with him many times this spring and enjoyed it well it was so pleasant.

Monona, July 12, 1853, Charlotte to Martha:

Thomas has him another fine horse and today has gone to Prairie Duchien for drugs.

Monona, December 1, 1853, Charlotte to Martha:

Another year has nearly run its round and perhaps before the close of another some of our number may pass away. I often think of it when I see one after another taken to the graveyard, several families are left to mourn the loss of some of its members. There has been several deaths from small pox in our neighborhood this fall. Some of congestion of the lungs, some of consumption, one man lost and perished on the prairie, so you see there is many ways of hastening us from time to eternity. Our little family still retain a state of tolerable health. Thomas still continues to ride. . . . He will not go out nights. His health will not admit of it. He surely has the consumption and there is no cure for him but he may live several years if he will take care of himself. . . . I am cross today you remember how ill-natured I can be, very like Mary Magdalene, I mean. I went with Thomas last night to see the sick, was kept up all night and today have the headache so that's all. [Thomas was ill for a time, but apparently cured himself, since in later letters there is no mention of this problem.]

Monona, March 1854, Charlotte to Martha:

Whilst I am now writing to you my head is nearly bursting with pain. I have not been undressed for 5 nights watching with Thomas. He has had a severe attack of jaundice. He is now better—been out to the meeting this forenoon but is quite feeble. I have no patience with him. He is so imprudent. His health is usually poor, but he is so ambitious he will keep about as long as he can breathe. I surely wish he would give up practice until his health is better, but he will go— get off his bed to visit persons that perhaps are no worse than himself.

. . . A great number have perished on the prairies this winter. One, Eddy, from Vermont, a brother of Thomas' brother-in-law was found dead a few days since and a young man that was with him has not been found yet. One girl twelve years of age perished a few rods from her home returning from school and was not found for four days. You have no idea of the blustering storms here. A person can not see any distance in the day and not many roads fenced and soon all traces of roads disappear and leave the poor traveller lost and bewildered.

Monona, June 10, 1855, Charlotte to Martha:

Thomas will be from home all night to see a dutchman with a broken skull, from fighting. Let him go, who cares. If the Devil was sick and sent for him he would surely go.

Monona, November 11, 1855, Charlotte to Martha:

Thomas was expecting to go away for Lectures at some Eastern Hospital this winter but has been too busily engaged to make any preparations.

. . . I went to meeting twice today. The new minister is preaching tonight but I will not go. Thomas is away as usual visiting the sick. He has no time for writing nor anything else. . . . Crops came in well this season but I can not tell you how much was raised on our place for the wheat is not threshed and the other grain is not measured. We can not brag about apples and cider—are compelled to use little nasty crab apples and go without cider for a treat but we live as well otherwise as anyone could wish. I have berries and plumbs and citrons for preserves, good dried apples and crabs for sauce so you see we live high. Beans, squash, turnip, potatos, beef and pork plenty. We will not starve yet. The teacher still boards with us and probably will till about Christmas. That change is mine 8/2 per week [8 shillings, 2 cents] and good company nights when Thomas is away.

Monona, July 15, 1857, Charlotte to Martha:

Thomas keeps going all the time most and complaining a great deal. His business is good and so is my health and Winfield's. . . . Francis is taking cod liver oil and bitter wild cherry prickly ash. If he gets better it will be as good a summer's work as he can do.

Monona, August 15, 1857, Thomas to Martha:

This is to tell you that our little one is well [Cora] but our Winfield is now dead. He died of flux and fever.

Monona, February 1858, Charlotte to Martha:

Poor husband has much to do, scarlet fevers, typhoid and "common complaints" plenty.

Monona, June 10, 1859, Charlotte to Martha:

I am just getting about from my sickness. I was confined the 27th of April and lost my child, a little Mary Elvira, but nevermind, all for the best, perhaps. . . . We will let the little "green grave" rest in the corner of our garden under a Locust tree. . . .

You know how unhappy I have felt about his [Charlotte and Martha's brother Francis] health . . . and have felt so anxious to have him come out here with us or have something done, but No, neglect to do anything, so 'fraid of doctoring only with herb tea. . . .

People are constantly on the move coming into our little town and building. The roads are full bound for Minnesota as many as 200 covered wagons in a day. Women and children, cattle, sheep and hogs. 'Tis a wonder where so many can find homes, but foxes have holes and birds have nests, so there must be habitation for the son of man. Our schools are in a flourishing condition. Sabbath school and church also.

Monona, September 1859, Charlotte to Martha:

Thomas is attending Lecture and doing first rate he thinks. He has left us comfortably situated as we could desire. . . . I have things of importance to look after, on the farm, collecting, writing letters, medical visits.

Monona, March 1860, Charlotte to Martha:

The winter has been mild, very little snow and that but a few days at a time. There is more sickness this winter than any winter since we have been here— fevers, the prevailing disease. Thomas is with the sick most of the time. He is getting well tired out. He is the only doctor in town.

Monona, August 24, 1862, Charlotte to Martha:

. . . Thomas was intending answering your letter but was called away 30 miles to visit cases of diptheria. The messenger said every case died. Thomas is so successful they sent a great distance for him. There was talk of having him surgeon in the army but the people can not do without him—if he is drafted he must hire a substitute.

BIOGRAPHICAL SKETCH

Monona, February 1863, Charlotte to Martha:

> Thomas has had quite a laborious winter. He has never had so much business since he commenced practice. There is no rest for him day nor night. The prevailing diseases measles, diptheria, lung fevers, typhoid fevers and that too common disease in new countries, increase of population.

Monona, April 1863, Thomas to Martha [on April 4, 1863, Charlotte died after a very short illness]:

> I must consider a while before I consent to have Charlotte's remains removed to your place for interment. I could ill remain at ease when thinking to the distant grave of my wife. My boy lies beside her and to their quiet places of repose I pay my respects and will bedew with my tears flowers that bloom over their graves.

Monona, September 6, 1865, Thomas to Martha:

> I am indeed finely situated as regards my pecuniary circumstances.

3

SUPERSTITIOUS WARNINGS OF IMMINENT DEATH

Death is deaf and hears no denials.
—Old proverb

One of the events recorded by Charles Baldwin, the Catskill stonecutter, was a poignant account of his daughter Etta's death from diphtheria and the fatal illness of his wife, Lizzie, which occurred at about the same time. Lizzie, lying ill in bed, must have had a premonition about the little girl, for, although folks at the time claimed it was impossible, she said she knew of Etta's death because she "saw the shadow of her coffin pass the chamber door."

Since ancient times the superstitious among us have listened to and believed, warnings of approaching death. There are phenomena about death that we do not understand, and just as certainly there are superstitions, which are ridiculous, but which some of us half believe. When I was a child and my Uncle

Clement Fuller was ill, I was terribly impressed to hear my mother say, "Clem won't live much longer. Aunt Jennie says he is picking at the bedclothes. Besides, a bird flew onto their front porch yesterday and tried to get into the house." This conversation probably stuck with me because Uncle Clem died in a few days, and I was left wondering what picking at the bedcovers and birds' getting into houses had to do with it.

Later, after Mother herself had been ill for several months, she asked to see me, telling my sister, "You know, I have only four hours left." That was at about eight in the evening. At midnight Mother died.

For centuries there has been a belief that birds are able to transport human spirits, which may underlie the widespread suspicion that birds carry the news of death. When President Andrew Jackson's niece, Emily Donelson, was ill, she sat one evening watching the sunset from her window. A bird flew in and fluttered about the room, circling, probably trying to find an exit. It finally lit on the back of Emily's chair, and one of her children ran to catch it. The child stopped at her mother's words, "Don't disturb it, Darling; maybe it comes to bid me prepare for my flight to another world." The child did not forget her mother's words, for within the week Mrs. Donelson died.

Two stories told to me by folklore pupils Candy Chadwick and Cheryl Malossi, respectively, are similar:

> My grandmother came over from Germany when she was young to work in a convent. One night as she lay in bed, a bird kept trying to get in through the window. She suspected the death of her father. The next day his death was confirmed.

> A mother sent her daughter to check on a baby she was caring for. When the daughter returned the mother asked anxiously for the infant.
> "He's very sick," said the girl.
> "No, Emma, he's dead," the mother said slowly. She elaborated, "A bird just came to the window and

tapped three times then flew away. I'm afraid he's dead, Emma."

Mother and daughter went back to the child's room. The baby was dead.

Bees as well as birds are associated with warnings of death. *Foxfire 2* tells about the incident of the "news bees" related originally by "Aunt Nora" Garland: "Well, now they's yeller ones—that's *good* news—and they's black ones, and that's *bad* news." She told of being pregnant, lying in bed for nine days before she delivered and watching a black news bee going in and out of her window. "It'd go out of the window and go right across toward the cemetery." The baby was born, died, and was buried over in the cemetery where the bee had flown.

These are a few of the strange warnings in which old-timers placed credence:

1. Beware if your rose blooms twice in the same year.
2. Be wary of a red rose that looks black. To prick your finger on one of its thorns means death.
3. If a dog howls at night when there is illness in the house, it is a bad omen. To counteract its ill effects, reach under the bed and turn over a shoe.
4. If a cow moos after midnight, it is an evil omen.
5. A white dove circling the house three times before lighting means death, but the victim will go to heaven. A pigeon circling the house before lighting means recovery for the patient.
6. A white moth inside the house or trying to enter means death.
7. Dreaming of a loved one lying in a coffin on one of the twelve nights immediately preceding Christmas warns of the death of that person during the coming year.
8. Never carry a shovel through the house. If you must take a shovel indoors, take it back out through the door by which you entered.

9. Footprints discovered in the ashes on the hearth when you first rise in the morning are a bad omen.

10. To see a tree blooming out of season means death.

11. To dream of a white horse signifies death.

12. To hear a hen crow means death, *unless* you kill the hen.

13. There will be a death in the family if a member dreams of muddy water.

14. To kill a lizard is a bad omen.

15. If a hearse stops while passing your house, it will choose its next victim from your house.

16. To see fire in the distance signifies death.

17. To see a light like a lighted candle moving about with no one holding it means death. This kind of light at night was referred to as a "corpse candle."

18. To dream of a sick person plowing is to anticipate the death of the person, *unless* he is plowing uphill. The latter signifies conquering the illness.

19. If the coffee grounds in the bottom of a cup form a long straight line, anticipate a funeral.

20. Overturning a loaf of bread in the oven means a death in the family.

21. If, when a rooster crows, all of the other roosters nearby also crow, it is a sign that a sinner is going to die.

22. Dropping an umbrella on the floor means that there will be a murder in that house.

23. A diamond-shaped fold in clean linen portends death.

24. Crossing knives at the table foretells death.

Abraham Lincoln told a peculiar story, which became significant in retrospect. He was discussing his first election to the presidency:

> It was after my election, when the news had been coming thick and fast all day, and there had been a great "hurrah, boys!" so that I was well tired out

and went home to rest, throwing myself upon a lounge in my chamber. Opposite to where I lay was a bureau with a swinging glass upon it; and, looking in that glass, I saw myself reflected nearly at full length; but my face, I noticed, had two separate and distinct images, the tip of the nose of one being about three inches from the tip of the other. I was a little bothered, perhaps startled, and got up and looked in the glass, but the illusion vanished. On lying down again I saw it a second time, plainer, if possible than before; and then I noticed that one of the faces was paler than the other. I got up and the thing melted away and I went off and in the excitement of the hour forgot all about it.

Lincoln went on to relate that once again he saw the double images but that afterward, when he tried to show his wife the phenomenon, he couldn't. Mary Lincoln was worried about the ghostly image and, in the President's words, "She thought it was a sign I was to be elected to a second term of office, and that the paleness of one of the faces was an omen that I should not see life through the second term."

Many folktales follow formulas; although they are told in different parts of the country or, perhaps, in different countries, they are often variations on the same theme. Here is an example of a formula story I have heard a number of times; only the place and people changed in each case.

Late one night I heard the doorbell ring. I went to the front door but no one was there. After a few minutes I heard a knock on the back door. When the door was opened, no one stood outside. About two hours after this I received a telegram saying that my sister had died a couple of hours before.

Another, more detailed story comes from northeastern New York State, from Westport on Lake Champlain. The *Troy*, an ore boat on its maiden voyage, had loaded its cargo at Port Henry and started north to its home port. It was November; the winds were cold and strong, and Lake Champlain, then as now, got very rough very fast. The ore must have shifted, for the ship foundered and sank somewhere near Barber's Point. All hands were drowned: the *Troy's* twenty-five-year-old captain, Jacob Halstead; his brother George; Jacob Pardee, their stepbrother; and two others. Father Halstead stood with friends on the wharf all night, watching. Parties started searching the shores at daybreak and found wreckage in Coll's Bay.

The Halstead women, though, knew before the debris was found that their menfolk would not come back alive. While they had sat around the fire at home, waiting with dry clothes and warm food for the boys, they had heard them arrive, open the door, and come into the entryway, stomping the snow off their boots as they came. The women hurried, relieved, to let them in. No one was there; the snow on the front steps and path was unmarred by footprints. The mother and her daughters turned toward each other in silence. They understood; the boys had tried to warn them what to expect.

In some stories the details are the opposite of those of the Westport tale; the people are seen but not heard. One of my pupils told about some people who were making ready for a guest, who was to arrive from out of town. They saw her coming down the street carrying her suitcase, dressed for the train trip she had just finished. They waited for her knock, but it never came. The explanation arrived later, a message that the would-be guest had died at home earlier that day.

The illusion of seeing someone who is not there is a rather common warning of death. Another story of this type involves a father and his son, who was killed in his early twenties in an auto accident. One Friday morning, three years after the boy's death, the father awakened to see his son standing at the foot of his bed. The gentleman thought he was dreaming. He closed his eyes, then opened them cautiously a second time. The boy still stood beside the bed, this time beckoning as if he wanted his father to follow him. The man closed his eyes a third time, trying to shut out the painful memory of his son's death. This time the illusion disappeared. Dressing quickly, the father hurried to tell his daughter what had happened. She listened carefully, surprised because her father seemed so shaken. Nothing more that was unusual happened that day or the next. On Sunday morning the father started for church as usual. He entered the sanctuary, nodded to friends as he walked down the aisle to an empty pew, knelt to pray, and died.

In another story a girl named Emma, her older married sister Ann, and the girls' uncle went blueberrying out along the edge of the woods. As they picked the ripe fruit, they strayed short distances from each other. Twice Emma thought she heard someone call, and she shouted to her uncle to ask if he wanted her. Each time he laughed and told her she was imagining things. They went back to the uncle's home. That night the girl was astonished when a man came into her room and put his arm around her shoulders, turning as if to speak to her. She recognized her brother-in-law's profile, but before she could speak, he disappeared. In the morning a message arrived announcing the death of Ann's husband.

Years back, the young son of a Virginia family went to sea against the entreaties of his mother. Laughingly he reassured her, saying that if anything ever went wrong he would let her know. A little over a year later, the mother was doing her housework when she heard a peculiar rapping and thumping above her. She searched for the cause of the sounds, following them up to the second floor and then into the garret. As she pushed up the trapdoor in the musty attic, she raised dust, which fell in a fine shower around her. The dust cleared and in the dimness she was startled to see her son, sitting on an old trunk smiling at her. The woman stared, and the illusion melted away as she watched, leaving the attic empty and the dust undisturbed. Apprehensive, she slowly descended the stairs, pondering the meaning of her vision. For a few days there was no answer to her questions, then a message arrived—her son had been the victim of an accident at sea.

Photographs, portraits, or other likenesses of persons not present have been involved in warnings of bad tidings. One evening a woman felt restless as bedtime approached, and after getting in bed she was unable to sleep. She confessed to her husband that she was worried about her uncle, afraid that something was about to happen to him. She dropped into a troubled slumber. Then a crash from the parlor awakened her and her husband. They hurried into their front room and found a framed photo of the uncle on the floor with its glass broken into fragments. There was little sleep for either of them the rest of that night. In the morning, when they inquired about the gentleman, their fears were justified. He was dead.

Amid flags waving and patriotic music blaring, parents sent a son off in uniform, and he went almost immediately into a battle zone. After he left his mother was startled one morning to hear the sound of a baby crying when she was alone in the house. As she searched the house, she stopped, noticing that the little rocker her son had used as a child was rocking by itself, empty. Notification of the boy's death in battle arrived shortly after that.

As a mother and daughter who had been watching at the father's bedside relaxed in the kitchen over cups of coffee, they heard sounds from the pantry, as if everything on the loaded shelves had been swept to the floor. Running into the room, they found nothing at all disturbed. "I guess there is only one explanation," the mother cried. "Hurry to your father. I'm afraid he is dead." She was right.

Here is a story in the words of a folklore student:

> When my grandfather was a young man, his mother died. At that time he was in a truck, far away, going in the opposite direction from his home. Out of nowhere he heard a voice that he recognized as his

sister's, saying, "Oh, no, Mamma!" In a quandary, he got in touch with his sister as soon as possible, only to find that he had heard the exact words she spoke when she realized their mother was dying.

Another student explained that she had had a disturbing experience:

> Three years ago my uncle died. Two or three weeks before he died, I had a dream. I dreamed I was sitting in a cemetery in front of a tombstone that had no name on it. There were four other people there but they didn't pay any attention to my questions about the missing name. I didn't think much about the dream until a few weeks after my uncle's death.
>
> Then I had the dream again, only it was much more vivid and complete this time. The tombstone had my uncle's name on it, and the four people sitting around it were my aunt and my three cousins.
>
> It's things like this that people wish they could know about before it was too late. I wish I could have realized whose name was going to be on that stone.

Have you ever heard of a chair spinning on one leg, seemingly unassisted? As a family sat around the kitchen while the grandmother was laying out newly washed clothes to dry, they talked together. Suddenly one of the chairs seemed to twirl around, then right itself. The first time this occurred, it was ignored. Then it happened again, and the elderly lady paled as she turned to the family.

"I wish that hadn't happened," she said. "You know, that's a sign that someone is going to die."

The someone proved to be a close relative, whose death shortly afterward justified the prophecy of the chair.

Several generations back a widow who had several children married a second time. Her new mate was plagued by two things: jealousy and a longtime habit of hitting the bottle when he was in difficulty. Despite that, the marriage went well at first; then the bridegroom found it harder and harder to support his new family, and he began, usually after a few drinks, to talk of suicide. No one took the threats very seriously until a summer evening when the man did not arrive home at his usual time. That night his wife and several friends sat on the porch, waiting up for him, hoping that nothing out of the ordinary had happened. They clustered comfortably around an old table, which had a kerosine lamp sitting in the middle, its wick turned low so that only enough light was shed on the faces to distinguish one from another. Suddenly there was a burst of flame, almost as if something inside the lamp chimney had exploded. The worried wife cried, "He's dead! It's a sign that he's dead!"

After a search of several days, the man's body was found in the old Erie Canal. No one ever knew whether he had wandered along the canal and fallen into the dark waters accidentally, or whether he had made good his oft-repeated threat. The police called it suicide and the case was closed. The memory of the exploding flame remained with those who had seen it whenever they sat outside in the dark of a hot summer evening.

Many Maine tales are associated with the sea. The setting for this one is a large comfortable farm home bustling with the activities of a large family. The maiden aunt who lived with the family was busily writing letters when she stopped to reread one and was startled to find a sentence she had no memory of writing. There in her script were the words, "Edward will die drowning." This was disturbing because Edward was the name of the oldest son, then at sea with his father. About a week later the news reached them. Edward, standing watch during a storm, had been washed overboard.

The family mourned the loss of this favorite son, but there was little change in their lives. After a few years another son was born, and he, after the custom of those times, was named Edward after his brother. When he was a few years old, his mother was called to help nurse a neighbor. As her husband was at work in the fields, she hitched the horse to the buggy herself and started down the lane. A hired hand hurried out to stop her, urging a quick return to the house. There she found the still form of her little Edward, whom the hired man had found face down in the watering hole. The name Edward was avoided in that family from then on. *Two* Edwards had "died of drowning."

Lights at night that have no explanation except for a timid suggestion of "will-o'-the-wisp" sometimes appear after death. According to one legend, a bluish light was frequently seen after a tragic accident beheaded a railroad worker. The light, they said, wended its way back and forth along the tracks as the ghostly body searched for its head.

Strange lights, the old wives say, also portend death. A mother and her small son were visiting relatives in the country. The mother happened to be just twice as tall as her fast-growing child. One evening as the mother and son were washing themselves in their upstairs chamber, they glanced out the window and noticed two lights moving along the country lane directly toward them. One light appeared to be twice as high from the ground as the other. The lights drew near, almost as close as the window from which the wide-eyed mother and her son were watching; then they drifted back and disappeared along the road at the foot of the hill, where the family burying ground had been fenced off. The rest of the household heard the bewildering story of the lights, and everyone searched for something that might have given off a peculiar reflection. Mirrors were moved, lights were shone in them, but nothing produced the peculiar effect described by the mother and her little boy. For a few days all was well. Then mother and son were suddenly taken ill. Just as suddenly, they worsened and died, and both were buried in the family plot into which the warning lights had disappeared.

Mrs. William Skidmore from Clapper Hollow near Schoharie, New York, received a warning she didn't understand. She was hurrying down her cellar stairs one morning, when she halted, forgetting her errand, at the sight of an open coffin at the foot of the stairs. Later in the day she heard of the death of a neighbor and remembered that the coffin she had seen was just his size.

One night, rather late, a man and his wife decided it was bedtime, although he did not expect to sleep well. A favorite sister was dangerously ill, and he had awaited a dread message all day. He undressed and lay silently awake, staring at the ceiling, remembering childhood days when a boy and girl lived and worked and enjoyed life back on the farm. Then he thought he saw a dim light against the ceiling and looked around to see what might be making the reflection. The light became brighter and brighter, circled the room, then was gone.

The man felt three taps on his shoulder and opened his eyes to see his wife entering the room. "Why did you do that? You startled me."

"Do what?" asked the puzzled woman.

"Tap me on the shoulder, when finally I had almost dropped off to sleep," he replied.

"But I didn't tap you on the shoulder," she explained. "I just came back into the room to tell you that a message has arrived. Your sister is dead."

> God calls his chosen home and
> Giveth his beloved sleep.
>
> —*Old epitaph*

4

FUNERAL CUSTOMS

Death devours lambs as well as sheep.
—Old proverb

Up in Jonesport, Maine, an old gentleman named Jeremiah, who had lived to be nearly one hundred, was upset when he overheard his wife sending the boys out to invite the neighbors to his funeral, which she figured would take place on the following Sunday. This was disturbing news to Jeremiah, and as he thought about it, he sniffed a tempting fragrance from the oven. "Marthy, Marthy, is them mince pies I smell a-bakin'?"

"Yes, Jeremiah, them's mince pies."

"Well, I think I'll have me a hunk."

"No, you won't, Jeremiah. I'm a-savin' them pies for your funeral!"

Funerals used to be more intimate than they are today. Even an invitation to a funeral was personal. In Dutch New Amsterdam and up the Hudson to Albany, the *aanspreecker*, or inviter, performed his own special service. Clothed in black, with long crape ribbons streaming from his hat, he hurried to the homes of relatives and friends of the deceased—for no one attended a funeral uninvited. By 1691 these Dutch "inviters to the buryiall of deceased persons" were public servants, appointed and licensed by a city's mayor. They were paid by the bereaved family according to the distance traveled and the length of time spent inviting, if the family could afford the service. If not, the *aanspreecker* made no charge. In 1682 in Flatbush, the inviter received twelve guilders per funeral, with an extra four guilders if he had to go into New York. By 1731 fees for the *aanspreecker* were set in English shillings: eighteen shillings for the funeral of anyone over twenty, twelve shillings for the funeral of a young person between twelve and twenty, and eight shillings for a child under twelve.

In Pennsylvania "warners" hustled off on horseback to notify friends of a death. Sometimes two dead-cakes, or *doed-Koecks* among the Pennsylvania Germans, a bottle of wine, and a pair of gloves were sent with the funeral invitation. The so-called

Note the skull and crossbones on this engraved undertaker's blank from the first half of the eighteenth century.

cakes were actually rather large cookies, made, according to an old recipe, from flour, sugar, butter, pearl ash salt, and caraway seed. According to tradition, they were not eaten but kept as a memento of the person who had died. The dead-cakes were often scratched with the initials of the deceased. Although usually baked in the home, in 1748 advertisements for such pastries could be found in Philadelphia newspapers.

The Moravians in Pennsylvania, unlike others of their German neighbors, were fond of singing and using instruments in their religious observances. They did not use an inviter but announced a death from the church bell tower where trombones played three chorales, the second indicating which choir the deceased had belonged to. Among Moravians, the word choir meant a group of people whose situations and interests were the same, such as a choir of widows or of little boys.

Among the Amish, friends told each other the news, but a death announcement was also displayed prominently on the village bulletin board.

By the second half of the nineteenth century, funeral invitations were printed on fine, small notepaper with a heavy black border and sent through the mail. This custom was especially prevalent in the more formal atmosphere of the city. (A collection of these somber notices is owned by the Historical Society of Montgomery County, Pennsylvania. The items date from 1838 to 1908.) The invitation followed a formula and was known variously as a ticket, a card, a notice:

> Yourself and family are respectfully invited to attend the funeral of Mr. James Hathaway from his late residence, 62 Bloom Street, Cherry Valley, on Monday, November 10, at 3 o'clock to proceed to Prospect Hill Cemetery.

A contemporary book of etiquette suggests:

> It is a breach of good manners not to attend a funeral when an invitation is sent. No calls of con-

dolence should be made upon the bereaved family while the dead remains in the house. All differences and quarrels must be forgotten in the house of mourning, and personal enemies who meet at a funeral must treat each other with respect and dignity. The bell knob or door handle is draped with black crape, with a black ribbon tied on if the deceased is married or advanced in years and with a white ribbon, if young or unmarried.

Almost as soon as there were bell towers on churches, the bells were used to toll an announcement of death. A verse reminds us:

> When the bell begins to toll,
> Lord have mercy on the soul.

This custom originated in Europe and at first was intended to frighten evil spirits waiting to capture the soul. Systems were worked out by some sextons to indicate the age and sex of the deceased. Some rang the bell once for a child, twice for a woman, three times for a man. Others rang it once for each year of the person's age. In small towns, where people lived in each other's hip pockets and everyone knew everything about his neighbors, it was usually easy to identify for whom the bell tolled.

In *Domestic Medicine*, Dr. Buchan bewails the tolling of bells, explaining:

> Many women have lost their lives in childbed by the old superstitious custom, still kept up . . . of tolling the parish bell for every person who dies. People who think themselves in danger are very inquisitive; and if they come to know that the bell tolled for one who died in the same situation with themselves what must be the consequence?

The death of a prominent person occasioned frequent public observances. When Rachel, wife of President Andrew Jackson, died, the Nashville City Council passed this resolution:

FUNERAL CUSTOMS

Resolved that the inhabitants of Nashville are respect-
fully invited to abstain from their ordinary business
on tomorrow, as a mark of respect for Mrs. Jackson,
and that the church bells be tolled from one until two
o'clock, being the hour of her funeral.

Toasts were raised in Rachel Jackson's honor, too, this one in
the Pennsylvania Legislature:

To the memory of Mrs. Jackson, the amiable wife
of the slandered hero. The grave now shrouds her
mortal remains, but her virtues will shine in brilliant
purity, when her unprincipled slanderers are lost to
the memory of man.

Many began plans for their own funerals early. Casks of wine
were put away, sometimes at the birth of a child, for *either* his
wedding or his funeral. In Albany, New York, the cask of
Madeira broken open for a gentleman's wedding was resealed to
be saved for his funeral feast. Special boards were also preserved
and kept in the attic for caskets when they should be needed.
When the Pennsylvania Germans were ready to build homes,
they planned a room called the *doed-kammer* or dead room,
where a body lay until time for the funeral. This room had
doors broad enough to allow the exit of bearers carrying a
casket. The rarely used parlor, always kept neat for a funeral or
a wedding, was found in many a New England home, too.

Linen shrouds with drawstrings at the top were woven tight
and bleached to a pure white, often to lie for years, yellowing
again with age, until they were discarded as no longer usable.

A couple of stories from the State of Maine remind us how
readily people used to accept death, how well adjusted they
seemed, how practical they were. One old-timer was dying and
knew it. A neighbor sat with him, talking to him, when the
sick man roused and spoke, "Lige, turn up the lamp and look in
the almanac—tell me when it will be high tide."

Order of Proceſsion,

for the FUNERAL of the late

GOVERNOR HANCOCK.

FUNERAL ESCORT,
under the Command of
BRIGADIER-GENERAL HULL.

OFFICERS of the MILITIA with ſide Arms,
JUSTICES of the PEACE,
JUDGES of PROBATE,
JUSTICES of the COURT of COMMON PLEAS,
ATTORNEY-GENERAL and TREASURER,
JUSTICES of the SUPREME JUDICIAL COURT,
MEMBERS of the HOUSE of REPRESENTATIVES,
MEMBERS of the SENATE,
SHERIFF of SUFFOLK, with his Wand,
MEMBERS of the COUNCIL,

Quarter M. Gen. }HIS HONOR THE
Adjt. General. } LIEUTENANT-GOVERNOR, } Secretary.

Aid de Camp   The Pall ſup-   Six of the eldeſt   Aid de Camp
to the deceaſed.   ported by   Counſellors.   to the deceaſed

RELATIONS.
VICE-PRESIDENT, and Members of CONGRESS,
JUDGES and SECRETARIES of the UNITED STATES,
Gentlemen heretofore Counſellors and Senators of Maſſachuſetts,
Foreign MINISTERS and CONSULS,
The PRESIDENT and CORPORATION,
The Profeſſors and other Inſtructors of HARVARD COLLEGE.
SELECTMEN and TOWN-CLERK,
OVERSEERS of the POOR and TOWN-TREASURER,
MINISTERS of the GOSPEL,
Members of the Ancient and Honourable ARTILLERY COMPANY.
Committee of Brattle-Street CHURCH, of which
the DECEASED was a Member.
other CITIZENS, and STRANGERS

Order of March.

The Proceſſion will move from the Manſion Houſe of the late
Governor HANCOCK, acroſs the Common—and down Frog-Lane,
to Liberty-Pole—through the Main-Street—and round the State-
Houſe—up Court-Street,—and from thence to the Place of Interment.

Colonel TYLER, will ſuperintend the forming of the Proceſſion of
Officers which precede the Corps.—and Col. WATERS. that of the
other Citizens who follow.

☞ It is deſired that the Proceſſion may move four a breaſt, when practicable.

New England had never seen a funeral as impressive as that of
John Hancock.

"She's a-goin' to turn in 'bout an hour, Cap'n."

"Well, in that case, you'd better go upstairs and get that punkin pine plank that all my forbears has been laid out on. I don't want a lot o' hollerin' goin' on here. 'Where's the board? Grandpa's slipped his cable.' "

Another fellow from Down East, Nathan Fisher, called his oldest son to his side. "James, go out and kill the fat lamb, so's the mourners'll have somethin' to eat after my funeral. And tell Mother to have supper jest as soon as the services are over so's the country folks can get back home by milkin' time."

A most unusual preparation ahead of time was a sermon preached by the deceased two weeks before she died. Aunt Nancy Range, mentioned in an earlier chapter as a "granny" in Pennsylvania, was a preacher, too. One Sunday she announced from the pulpit that on the next meeting day she would preach her funeral sermon. (She claimed to have a premonition that she would not live long.) Of course the congregation flocked from every direction, and the people were not disappointed; Aunt Nancy presented one of her finest orations. Her premonition, too, was accurate; she died within two weeks.

Another example of considerate preparation in anticipation of death involves George Carver, a common laborer and an uncommonly generous and thoughtful gentleman of Saranac Lake in New York's Adirondacks. George, who died only a couple of years ago at seventy-two, was a devout man who bought a Cadillac sedan so he could take the sisters from nearby convents about their business and pleasure "in style." Mr. Carver picked out the clothes he wished to be buried in and hung them, labeled, in his closet. He also dug his own grave in a rocky, hard-to-shovel part of the cemetery and then filled it with sand so that it could be shoveled out easily.

Proper burial clothes seem to have been the concern of many. In Emelyn Gardner's *Folklore from the Schoharie Hills*, mention is made of a visit to the local poor farm, where every mattress in the women's section held burial clothes, all pressed in readiness for the "handsome funeral" each hoped for.

The same source quotes the marvelous conversation of Betsey Bouck from Middleburgh, New York, who discusses her difficulties with a "witch" and is reconciled because of happy anticipation of her own funeral.

> I have seen a lot of trouble in my time. Most of it was the work of old Miss Schemerhorn, too. I used to keep a trout in my well, but a trout couldn't do anything against such as her. Then I tried fish in my spring, because I thought, being higher up, they could see her doings and help me. But, land sakes, she fixed them in no time, and they sickened and died on me. My pig died, my colt died, and Old Schemerhorn sent such a blast of wind one day that my only good apple tree, a sapsunvine, just split all to bits, and there was nothing left of it but the stump you can see there. I tell you, I've had trouble that's trouble and only the poor farm's ahead for me. But I've got good clothes to be buried in. It's a wonder Old Schemerhorn didn't claw them to ribbons. She was capable of it! But it's comforting to think that when I'm laid out I'll look just as good as the best. I've got a black silk dress made so 'twon't show if I am wasted as most dead be. And I've laid away a wool underskirt with a silk ruffle on and nice underclothes with lots of crocheted lace on.

There is another story of preparation for death ahead of time that has a strange ending. It features a prosperous horse trader in upper New York who had acquired considerable wealth. He had a vision in which he was told that he would die in his own bed on a specified date. Zeb laid aside a good supply of hard cider for the funeral and planned his last days carefully. The time neared and the "hoss trader" felt poorly. He took to his bed, and friends and relatives gathered to be there at the end. As the dreaded hour approached, his cronies tried to keep up a conversation but fell into long silences when they could think of nothing to say. The women became hysterical and two of them fainted.

As the clock struck twelve, the appointed hour, the tearful wife sent two men to lay out the corpse. They were surprised by a white-robed, wild-eyed apparition, whom they finally recognized as Zeb, still alive.

He explained that as he lay there listening to his own death rattle, a woman in black had appeared before him, smiling and saying, "Arise, friend, I am the way and the light. Follow me and you shall be saved. Watch and I will come." The woman disappeared. Zeb insisted that he had never seen her before, but that he would know her at once when he saw her again.

Rejoicing replaced the atmosphere of apprehension and gloom. The menfolk finished the barrel of hard cider thoughtfully provided by their host and invited him down to the tavern, where a hilarious wake was held.

His narrow escape from the jaws of death had a peculiar effect on the horse trader. His interest in business fell off. He became absentminded around home and less appreciative of his wife's devotion. There was only one thing on his mind: finding the woman in black.

As he drove past the cemetery one morning, Zeb saw a wagon approaching, its horse driven by a pale woman in mourning. Behind her in the open wagon was a coffin with two young men sitting on it.

Zeb's pulse beat faster, for he recognized his deliveress. He followed her into the burying ground. The widow did not seem at all surprised to see him, and commented simply, "So you are here already. I knew it would take four to lower the coffin."

Zeb stumbled down from his buggy, so excited he could hardly stand. He assisted the young men, obviously brought along just to help with the burying, and, after shoveling earth back into the grave, escorted the woman home. From that time on, he never left her. He did not return to explain to his family, to gather up a few possessions, to say farewell. It was as if he were bewitched, and his wife believed he was. She swore vengeance on the "witch woman," which was what the horse trader's former friends called this Pied Piper who had lured him away from home and family.

And perhaps Mrs. Zeb had vengeance, for when the lovers were buggy riding one fine afternoon, the woman in black fell from the vehicle, rolled down a steep precipice, and sustained several serious cuts. The scars were so disfiguring that she never appeared in public again, and she and Zeb lived out their lives together in apparently happy isolation.

A touching story was related recently by the proprietor of a dress shop, who told my husband and me that he'd just had a customer desiring "a black dress to wear to a funeral." When the woman had found one she liked, she asked if she might wear it outside to show her husband, who was waiting in the car. After doing this she returned to the shop to pay for the outfit, explaining that the dress was for her husband's funeral. He was suffering from a terminal illness, and since they usually did things together, they had come to pick out her funeral costume.

Funerals used to be performed soon after death, since there were few attempts at embalming in America until after the Civil War. In winter, when the ground was frozen, all sorts of make-do practices evolved. According to a New Hampshire native, folks inconsiderate enough to die in wintertime were buried in their coffins under the snow up in the spruce woods. The problem, according to the storyteller from New Hampshire, was to re-member where the coffins were when the spring thaw came.

When I was a child, my father took our family into the Adirondack backcountry, off the beaten track past Paul Smith's to an abandoned mining village, where only one man and his wife still lived. Uncle Joe was a hunter and trapper. He and his wife lived on what they could make serving "wild beef" to tourists, who came in at twilight to watch the deer at their salt lick.

Later we heard that Joe had died in midwinter, when Mrs.

The simplicity of a prairie burial was in keeping with the style of life led there.

Joe couldn't even get a message out. She moved Joe's body into a back room, the summer kitchen, laid him out there, and allowed the body to freeze, so it would keep until spring, when an undertaker could be reached.

Abner Eyde, quoted in "Lancaster City Boy," also notes, "I've heard that it was common in old times to tie the body onto a cooling board and hang it in the barn until the spring ground thaw." A cooling board often became the resting place of the corpse until the coffin was completed, since the sick bed was probably needed for visiting relatives.

Southern Negroes, like many others, used a cooling board for laying out their dead and, in the past, placed a plate of salt and ashes beneath the board. The ashes were put there to absorb disease and, at the committal service, were placed in the grave.

Everyone is familiar with the custom of burial at sea. Occasionally, though, there was either a special desire or a real need to preserve the body of one who died there. This presented a challenge. Ingenuity usually won, and in several instances bodies were successfully preserved in alcohol. Lord Nelson, the British naval hero, was reputedly returned to England from Trafalgar in a keg of rum.

An American privateer was happy to encounter the ship of a notorious pirate. During the battle between the pirates and the crew of the American ship, the pirate leader was killed. There was a bounty on his head, and the American captain took it literally. He pickled the bandit's head in alcohol, so he could return home, exhibit his trophy, and claim the reward.

For years, longer in the country than in the cities, it was the custom for neighbors to wash and prepare the dead for burial.

Laying out among the Amish was performed by two members of the same sex as the deceased. The women were dressed in white: cap, kerchief, dress, and apron; the men, in white shirts and black suits.

One source I've read says male corpses were not dressed in

A preacher delivering the eulogy over a coffin.

trousers. Expensive winding sheets, less expensive shrouds, or other special garments provided by the mortician were in common use by everyone until 1900. By then men were apt to be garbed in a commercial covering with a dickey and tie but a shirtlike bottom. Women have frequently been dressed in their wedding gowns, saved, like wine, from wedding to funeral.

A niece of the Thomas Jeffersons was living in their home when one of Mrs. Jefferson's sisters died. The young girl wrote that when she visited the chamber where her aunt lay, "the body was covered by a white cloth, over which had been strewn a profusion of flowers." Sometimes the coffin was placed in the chamber on the deceased's bed, rather than in the parlor.

A Philadelphia directory for 1810 lists fourteen women as "Layers out of the Dead." One of the first competitors to take over any of the tasks that eventually fell to the undertaker was the carpenter or cabinetmaker who provided the coffin. David Evans of Philadelphia, a cabinet and coffinmaker, listed in his daybook:

> Sept. 7, 1780: Estate of William Allen, late Chief Justice, making his Coffin of Mahogany, with Plate, horse hire, and attendance on the corpse from Mount Airy, £13.

> Aug. 2, 1798: Estate of Col. Innes—making him Mahogany Coffin, Plate, Handles and Lace £15. My attendance bringing the corpse from the country £1 10. Muslin for Winding Sheet £1 10.

Along with the cabinetmaker, the livery-stable keeper who provided the hearse and carriages and the sexton who tolled the bell and dug the grave might share in additional services for the dead. An advertisement from Cambridge, New York, reads: "Z. Cotton & Sons, Undertakers, Dentists, Picture Frames a Specialty." Charlestown, Massachusetts, advertised that it had its own local undertaker in 1838, Thomas Knight of 8 Austin Street. An

1859–1860 Lancaster, Pennsylvania, directory lists three undertakers: Anne Conrad, Jr., Mary Hoffman, and Mary Miller.

Thomas Holmes has been called the father of modern embalming. Born in 1817 in New York City, he practiced his art during the Civil War, especially upon officers killed in battle whose families hoped to get them home for burial. After the war he attempted a private practice in Washington, D.C. Apparently his services were not in great demand there, for he returned to Brooklyn and a career as doctor-druggist-embalmer to continue his experiments concocting fluids of varying potency and purpose, including an especially tasty root beer!

A Western gunman called Johnny Eldorado was thoroughly prepared in case his luck should run out. Johnny aspired to become top man around the Comstock Lode and went out gunning for his chief opponent, Langford Peel. The desperado knew that Farmer Peel was tough, and Johnny wasn't at all sure of the outcome of his challenge. Therefore, he visited the barber for a shave. He then asked the barber to curl his hair and the bootblack to shine his shoes. Dressed in his best, he swaggered down the street to confront Peel. The latter killed Johnny handily, but Johnny's preparations paid off. He was carted off to the cemetery with ceremony as the hometown band played "When Johnny Comes Marching Home Again," and was known for years as the most elegant corpse the local ruffians had ever buried.

Preparedness, though, can be overdone. There was an elderly fussbudget whose husband often had to travel on business. Whenever he went on a long trip, she packed his "laying out" clothes in case he should die while he was away.

Frequently folks have decided opinions about the treatment of their own corpses, and over the years they have given some especially peculiar instructions concerning the matter. John Reed, who served for forty-four years as gaslighter in the Walnut Street Theater in Philadelphia, became singularly attached to that theater. He served it well—never absent from a performance, never tardy. Reed wanted to be represented, permanently, at the theater. Accordingly, in his will he asked that his head be separated from his body immediately upon death and that his body be buried and his head prepared "to be brought to the theater where I have served all of my life, to be employed to represent the skull of Yorick in the play *Hamlet*."

Another request was even stranger; one gentleman left his body to the Harvard Anatomical Museum, asking that two drumheads be covered with his skin. One was to be inscribed with Pope's "Universal Prayer," the other with the Declaration of Independence. The drums were to be forwarded to a friend in Cohasset, who was a drummer. Annually on July 17, the friend was asked to use the drums to beat the rhythms of "Yankee Doodle" at the foot of Bunker Hill.

In 1815 William White, who had been a soldier during the War of 1812, lay abed in his cabin in Brokenstraw Valley, near Pittsfield, Pennsylvania. His neighbors watched over him, plying him with nourishing food, knowing he had been feeble since his return from the war, and hoping they'd be able to conquer his fever and build up his strength. They kept his curtains pulled and the windows shut tight, as was the custom of the day, but White seemed only to grow weaker. Finally he lapsed into a coma and after a while appeared dead. No pulse could be felt; when a mirror was held to his lips, no beads of moisture could be seen. White's friends mourned his death, but decided to air out his chamber before laying him out. They pushed the curtains apart, flung open the windows, and went into the kitchen to heat water and have some food before starting their task. On their return to the bedroom, a friend noticed that White looked different; as they checked more carefully, an eyelid fluttered. With fresh air and sunshine the man had revived! He recovered from his near-fatal fever and lived for years.

Such a sudden return from the dead has happened more than once. The following story is quoted just as I first read it from an undated newspaper clipping in an old scrapbook:

Paul Pelkey of Fillmore, Missouri, is still living and is 102 years old. He took sick and died 40 years ago, was dressed in grave clothes, and was placed in a coffin in an upstairs room at his home. The funeral was ready to start, and the stairs were very narrow and old-fashioned, and but two men could handle the coffin. They started down the stairway with the coffin, and one of the men slipped, and down went the coffin, bumpety bump. The coffin broke open, and the corpse sat up and rubbed his eyes and asked for a drink of water, and Paul Pelkey's funeral was put off indefinitely and has not since been announced, and it is said is not likely to be for some time to come.

When the termagant wife of a mild-mannered deacon died, a quick burial was arranged. As bearers carried the coffin into the tomb, one slipped, and the box hurtled against a wall. There was an immediate cry, "Let me out!" In shocked silence, the bearers opened the coffin. The "corpse" shook her fist at the deacon as he tried to raise her from her cramped quarters. Despite the remonstrances of the deacon and the bearers, who promised to take her back the same way she had come, the woman insisted on adding to the neighborhood scandal by walking home in her burial clothes. When in about six months the deacon's wife really succumbed, her husband had a private talk with the sexton and bearers, reminding them of the "sad turn" things had taken at the first burial. They all solemnly agreed to proceed *very* carefully and were promised a treat at the deacon's store the day *after* a successful interment.

Another wife became an embarrassment to her husband because she was much too fond of hard cider. When his threats failed to cure her, he tapped a new, full barrel and invited her to drink her fill. She did, and collapsed. When she didn't revive, it was decided her hard drinking had finally done her in. Her funeral was arranged, and she was buried in the family tomb. The cold tomb, however, revived the woman, and the sexton, about to seal the tomb, heard entreaties from below: "Good

84

people of the upper world, if ye have got any good cider, do let us have a mug of it." To her husband's chagrin, the sexton felt obliged to release the wife from her prison.

It has been the custom among Irish Catholics to watch over the body of a loved one between the time of death and the time of burial. This custom is not exclusively Irish or Catholic; in older times, many followed this practice. Folks sat in relays, daytime and nighttime, and in earlier days, if the weather was hot, kept fresh cloths soaked in vinegar over the hands and face of the dead.

One night an elderly gentleman was sitting with the body of a man who had been a friend, and he dozed as the night grew late. The body was not yet enclosed in a casket; it had been placed on the laying-out board with boards laid carefully on top to keep the limbs straight. Suddenly there was a loud noise as one of the boards clattered to the floor. It appeared to the sleepy watcher that the corpse had kicked off the weight. The man's shouts brought others to examine the body. They decided that the leg muscles had contracted to jar the board from its position. Their friend had not come back to life, and from then on he lay quite still.

Some Irish wakes used to become spirited parties, and upon occasion the corpse was stood up in the corner to enjoy (as best he might) the revelries. In North Norwich, New York, friends of two Irish railroad men were invited to their wake. The railroad workers, Mike and Jim Gavin, in their cups, had commandeered a handcar and careered down the track to meet a fast passenger train head-on. Jim was beheaded and Mike, according to local gossip, "so smeared over the wheels they had to scrape him off with a case knife." Comrades of the two men celebrated the accident appropriately with a rousing, rowdy farewell party, at which they removed Jim's head from the coffin and set it on a high chair with his favorite pipe hanging from the corner of his mouth.

Actually this party in the late 1800's was little different from

A family fighting over the inheritance at a wake in nineteenth-century New York.

earlier funeral revelries. Records relate that in 1756 Lucas Wyngard died in Albany, was buried, and his funeral feast begun. This became an all-night celebration and free-for-all. A pipe of wine was drunk, dozens of pounds of tobacco were smoked, grosses of clay pipes were used and smashed, and not a whole glass or decanter remained in the house by morning. The pallbearers finally kindled a fire in the fireplace with the scarves they had been given as tokens of their office.

Nathaniel Hawthorne commented on the attitude of old New Englanders at the time of a death in their community. "They were the only class of scenes . . . in which our ancestors were wont to steep their tough old hearts in wine and strong drink and indulge in an outbreak of grisly jollity." And Thomas Hunt, who wrote *Wedding Days of Former Times* published in 1845, lamented:

FUNERAL CUSTOMS

I knew a father once who, at the birth of his eldest daughter procured a large assortment of intoxicating liquors, which he declared should not be used until her death or marriage. . . . For in those days, liquors, cakes and drunkenness were often seen at funerals. . . . Both rich and poor alike felt that the funeral arrangements were as incomplete without liquor as without a hearse or coffin. Fathers have been known to stagger to the grave, husbands to fall down and sons to be drunken at the burial of all that is dear.

A bill summing up expenses after the drowning of David Porter in Hartford, Connecticut, in 1678 lists:

pint of liquor for those who dived for him	1	shilling
quart of liquor for those who brought him home	2	”
2 quarts of wine and 1 gallon of cyder to jury of inquest	5	”
8 gallons and 3 quarts of wine for funeral	15	”
Barrel of cyder for funeral	16	”
1 coffin	12	”
winding sheet	18	”

Callie Dawes died in Boston in 1797, and the funeral feast again was the greatest expense. Rum, wine, gin, beer, and brandy were served along with beef, ham, bacon, fowls, fish, oysters, eggs, peas, onions, potatoes, cheese, fruit, and sweetmeats—at a cost of $844.

⌈A Lutheran gentleman from Pennsylvania wrote, "Our Germans look forward all of their lives to their funerals, hoping to be able to entertain their friends on that great occasion with the hospitality due them."⌋ At Dutch funeral feasts all kinds of goodies were offered: stewed chicken, ham, cold meats, cheese, mashed potatoes, applesauce, red beets, pie, and coffee. The pie was probably raisin or *leicht boi,* known throughout Pennsylvania and New England as "funeral" pie. If someone was ill and there seemed little hope of his recovery, the remark "There'll be raisin pie yet" was certain to be heard.

In good weather in Pennsylvania Dutch country, tables were set out under the trees as well as in the house and in the threshing barn. Old men and women sat at the first table with the close mourners. Eddie Sussekuche, who lived in Lebanon, attended all of the funerals he could reach for the sake of the funeral feast. There was a saying around there that "A funeral's not a funeral without a corpse and Eddie Sussekuche."

The first recorded death in Marietta, Pennsylvania, in 1807, was that of a twelve-year-old boy named Walton. The ceremony was conducted in the front yard of the house while the bearers stood by the bier. Afterward two people with large trays covered with white linen passed among the guests and offered them cheese, sweet cake, wine, and Jamaican rum.

Cornelius Weygandt attended a Mennonite funeral in upper Bucks County. A man had been murdered near his home, and there was a large funeral attendance. It was a six-mile drive from the home, where the funeral took place, to the church, where the victim was buried, and the long procession of wagons took two hours to traverse the six miles. When the mourners arrived, they found that "great copper kettles swung by chain and trammel from stout saplings laid across between the lower limbs of oaks and hickories of the meetinghouse grove and long fires of logs were burning beneath the kettles. There was coffee for all." Among the "plain folk," intoxicating beverages were not used, but after the burial folks gathered around the steaming pots with cakes, doughnuts, and sandwiches, so that the whole grove, according to Weygandt, "resembled Thanksgiving Day."

The first death among the Brethren of the Ephrata Cloister occurred in 1738; it was that of the community tailor, Brother Martin Bremmer. Immediately after Martin died, his cabin window was opened so that, according to the beliefs of the Brethren, his soul could fly heavenward unhindered. The Cloister bell was tolled, and plans were made for burial after the Brethren's usual midnight service.

As Bremmer's body was carried from the house, a bucket of water was splashed over the doorsill and swept outward. The door was closed at once to keep the spirit of Brother Martin from reentering, and three crosses were marked on the doorjamb with red clay.

When Brother Conrad Beissel, founder of the community, died in 1768, the Sisters informed the hives of bees, according to the old superstition, so that they wouldn't swarm. Every barrel, keg, or crock of wine, pickles, kraut, vinegar, and preserved fruit was turned bottom side up to prevent spoilage. For years, among these Americans of German extraction, it was also traditional, when the mother of a household died, to send someone to the cellar to shake the vinegar bottle, in an attempt to wake the *essich-mutter*, the mother of vinegar.

Amish funerals were always held in the home and were exceedingly simple; there were no flowers, no crape, and no embalming until the latter was required by law. All attending the funeral wore black, friends along with relatives. Four friends—single if the deceased was single, married, if he was married—were selected as bearers, and their duties included more than the term usually implies. These four helped at the home to get everything in readiness, carrying benches from the meetinghouse and, with a team of womenfolk, "redding up" the house. They dug the grave and filled a farm or Conestoga wagon with hay to convey the coffin to the grave.

The funeral itself included an introductory sermon, a silent prayer, reading from the Scripture, the main sermon (which was *not* a eulogy), a prayer from the prayer book, and a benediction. The preacher led the procession from the home to the burying ground with church bells tolling en route. At the cemetery the four who had been chosen previously lowered the coffin and filled in the grave. When this had been completed, the minister read a hymn, said a few more words, then gave the benediction. Modern Amish burials are still much like those of their forebears.

A story is told of the leisurely ride home to Reading by carriage of four chosen "helpers" after a burial. In this instance one was older than the others.

Youngest man: "Charlie, how old are you?"

Charlie: "Seventy-nine."

Youngest man: "Seventy-nine! H'mm. Hardly worth while carrying you home."

The decorated baptismal certificate or *Taufschein*, often used to be placed with the body in the coffin; in Lehigh County it was sometimes laid under the tombstone. Some people have suggested that the tradition started with the belief that this paper was a sort of "passport to Heaven."

In Lititz, a fear of contagion kept the deceased out of the sanctuary, so the Moravian people provided a special "corpse house," where bodies were laid. The pall over the coffin was white, sometimes with blue embroidery. During the funeral they sang hymns; a band led the funeral procession.

In Warwick Township mourners sat around the coffin, which had been loaded into a straw-lined wagon, and rode that way to the cemetery. At the cemetery they again encircled the coffin, and partook of wine and cake together. These people did not feel that it was necessary to dress elaborately for a funeral and usually left off their work to attend the services in their working clothes.

In the Lancaster, Pennsylvania, area, when high beaver hats were the vogue, male mourners wore them to funeral services, to the indignation of the ladies.

Funerals among the Scotch-Irish were simple. Burial was in a family plot after a service at home. As with the Amish, the coffin was provided by the local carpenter, and the grave was dug by friends, who also brought around a wagon if the roads permitted it. When the roads were muddy, the coffin was slung on poles and carried by four husky men. Unlike the Amish, the Scotch-Irish did not provide a feast, although a jug may have been passed around.

Funerals in the Southern states were major social events. Although plantations were far apart, an effective means of spreading news had been worked out. When there was a death, the family concerned notified four neighbors; in turn, these four neighbors let their immediate neighbors know what had happened. In this way, the news was carried for a fifty-mile radius. Guests came by carriage if roads permitted, by horseback if not. While they were assembling, cake was served on large tin "waiters," or trays, along with hot West Indian rum punch. The punch was made from rum plus sugar, lemon juice, and juniper berries, and was served in goblets. Hot sweetened cider was also offered to the guests. After a traditional funeral service, the mourners followed the coffin to the place of burial, with perhaps as many as five hundred people on horseback. Gun salutes were sometimes fired over the grave.

Fortunately travelers were apt to recount funeral customs; without their accounts many old customs might have been lost. The journal of the Reverend John Taylor, who toured the central part of New York in 1802 and visited at Tribe's Hill along the Mohawk, tells us rather bluntly:

> . . .⌈The High Dutch have some singular customs with regard to their dead. When a person dies, nothing will influence ye connections, nor any other person, unless essentially necessary, to touch the body. When the funeral is appointed, none attend but such as are invited. When the corpse is placed in the street, a tune is sung by a choir of singers appointed for the purpose—and continue singing until they arrive at the grave; and after the body is deposited, they have some remarks made—return to ye house, and in general get drunk. Twelve men are bearers—or carriers —and they have no relief. No will is opened, nor debt paid, under six weeks from ye time of death.⌋

It was not considered proper for women to walk in a funeral procession, so the ladies usually stayed at the home of the deceased, eating cookies and sipping Madeira and burnt wine in silver tankards while their menfolk went to the cemetery.

The paternal attitude of the New York Dutch toward their poor was admirable. As an example, in 1696 the Widow Ryseck Swart transferred her worldly possessions —her silver, a strip of pasture land, and a few pieces of jewelry—valued at about three hundred guilders, to her church in Albany. From that time the church elders provided for her necessities and her well-being, and paid Marritje Lievertse thirty-six guilders a month to look after the widow, who lived until February 1700 at a cost to her fellow churchmen of about 2,229 guilders. On top of that, she was given a proper funeral, and an appropriate feast was served for those who mourned her death. The bill has been preserved:

	Guilders
3 dry boards for coffin	7
¾ of a pound of nails	1
Charge for making coffin	24
Cartage	10
Half a vat and anker of good beer	27
1 gallon of rum	21
6 gallons of Madeira for women and men	84
Sugar	5
150 sugar cakes	15
Tobacco and pipes	5
Use of pall	10
Wife Jans Lockermans	36

[Jans Lockermans probably laid out the widow.]

There was a time when gifts were passed out so freely, as mementos of the dead, that the expense was overwhelming. This

Photographs of the deceased with the family gathered around were popular.

custom was practiced particularly in New England and among the Holland Dutch. In 1721 a law was passed in Massachusetts making it illegal to give lavish gifts at funerals, and both during and after the Revolutionary War, fines were enacted against those who spent extravagantly for the last rites of their relatives. There were to be no gifts, no "spirituous liquors" served, no new mourning clothes purchased for the gentlemen, except for black armbands. The ladies were allowed only new bonnets, gloves, fans, and black ribbons.

Nevertheless, when the wife of Governor Belcher died in 1736, in the Massachusetts Bay Colony, over a thousand pairs of gloves were given away. Andrew Eliot, pastor of the famed North Church in Boston, tallied up the gift gloves he had acquired over thirty-two years and found he had 2,940 pairs. Samuel Sewell had fifty-seven mourning rings, and when Dr. Samuel Buxton of Salem died in 1758, his heirs found a quart tankard filled with funeral jewelry. One fifth of Waitstill Winthrop's estate went to pay for sixty funeral rings valued at over a pound apiece, scarves, gloves, tailor's bills, and bell tolling for the funeral.

Death among the Dutch patroons along the Hudson was a time of particular expense, since all of the tenants on the patroonship were included in the feasts and were the recipients of gifts. When Philip Livingstone died in 1749, there were services and festivities both in his town house in Manhattan and at the manor in the country. Visitors in the city enjoyed spiced wine and tobacco. The bearers received gloves, rings, scarves, handkerchiefs and "apostle spoons," which were so named because of the crude portraits on the handles. At the manor different bearers received the same gifts, and all the tenants were given black gloves and handkerchiefs. The whole expense reached five hundred pounds.

It is easier to understand the tradition of presenting a gift to someone who nursed the deceased than it is to understand wholesale gift giving at a funeral. Quite often one or two silver spoons were conferred in appreciation of nursing care by a neighbor. These may be the spoons that are referred to as "coffin spoons." They were frequently put to practical use, being hung on the post of a cradle for an infant to teethe on.

A contemporary gives us a picture of a typical scene at a country funeral of the 1800's:

⌐Everyone as he entered, took off his hat with his left hand, smoothed down his hair with his right, walked up to the coffin, gazed down upon the corpse, made a crooked face, passed up to the table, took a glass of his favorite liquor, went forth upon the plat before the house, and talked politics, or the new road or compared crops, or swapped heifers or horses, until it was time to lift.⌐

In Philadelphia a gentleman named Dr. Cutter reported seeing one Sunday six men, walking two and two toward church, wearing "very large white sashes made of fine Holland, the whole width, and two or three yards long." Each sash was over the right shoulder and tied under the left arm in a large bow. Several yards of white ribbon streamed from the top of the shoulder, and a large ribbon rose had been fashioned and fastened on the sash. As the doctor watched, the six men met the minister, who was wearing a black sash in the same manner. Upon inquiry Dr. Cutter found that these ornamental sashes had been worn earlier in the week at the funeral of "a person of note," and that it was the custom to appear at church the Sunday following such an elaborate ceremony wearing the same funeral regalia.

One funeral custom, which seems inhumane, was the use of young bearers when the deceased was a child. One such incident has been recorded as happening in Concord, New Hampshire. The little corpse was borne on a chaise with six little bearers walking beside it, the oldest no more than twelve. Before they left their friend's home for the cemetery, one of their elders mixed for each of them a tumblerful of gin, water, and sugar.

Two diaries add details about the use, also, of young women as bearers. Miss Sarah Eve wrote in 1772: "In the evening B. Rush, P. Dunn, K. Vaughn and myself carried Mr. Ashe's child to be buried; foolish custom for Girls to prance it through the streets without hats or bonnets!" (The Ashe child was Rebecca, second child of Colonel James Ashe, who married three times and fathered twenty-four children.)

Hannah Wharton noted on December 19, 1813:

> We have had a melancholy occurrence in the circle of our acquaintances . . . in the death of the accomplished and amiable Fanny Durdin. Six young ladies of her intimate acquaintance, of which I was one, were asked to be the pall bearers. We were all dressed in white with long white veils.

From "Lancaster City Boy," undertaker Abner Eyde adds:

> Often when we embalmed children who'd died of diphtheria we'd be asked to hold them up to a window so their playmates could get a last look. Not allowed to have viewings. Then we'd wrap the body in a sheet soaked in formaldehyde, then in cotton, then in another sheet. If it was buried outside of the city the casket had to be put in a tin box and the tinsmith had to solder all the edges. State law.

Lancaster, Pennsylvania, boasts the first crematorium built in America, in Cedar Lawn Cemetery in 1884. When the service was established, the cost of cremation included twenty-five dollars for two hundred pounds of steamboat coke and an attendant, ten dollars for the undertaker furnishing a cheap casket, five dollars for the hearse, and three dollars apiece for carriages for the mourners.

Here are a few of the many superstitions relevant to the dead:

FUNERAL CUSTOMS

1. If a dead person's eyes are left open, he will find a companion to take with him.

2. Place a quarter in the coffin of a dead person so he can pay his toll across the River Jordan.

3. If several deaths occur in the same family, tie a black ribbon to everything left alive that enters the house, even dogs and chickens. This will protect against death's spreading further.

4. Pull the shades at a funeral. If the sun shines on the face of a mourner, he will be the next to die.

5. Cover mirrors in a house where there is a corpse. The person who sees himself may be Death's next victim.

6. Never allow a child under the age of one to attend a funeral.

7. Do not attend a funeral if you are pregnant.

8. It is bad luck for a bride and groom to meet a funeral procession.

9. Do not wear anything new to a funeral, especially shoes.

10. A corpse must be taken from the house feet first. If his head faces backward, he may beckon another member of the family to follow him.

11. If the deceased has lived a good life, flowers will bloom on his grave; if he has been evil, weeds will grow.

12. It is bad luck to meet a funeral procession head-on. If you see one approaching, turn around.

13. Never arrange a Friday funeral. This is apt to mean another death in the family during the year.

14. A person who transplants a cedar tree will die when the lower limbs of the tree reach the length of his coffin.

15. If a broom is rested against a bed, the person who sleeps there will soon die.

16. Taking ashes out of a stove after sundown will bring a death in the family.

17. A person who sees thirteen white horses at the same time will soon be carried in a hearse.

18. Large drops of rain warn that there has just been a death.
19. Count the cars of a passenger train, and you will hear of a death.
20. Stop the clock in a death room, or you will have bad luck.
21. You will have bad luck if you meet a white chicken when you are on your way to a funeral.
22. To lock the door after a funeral procession has left the house is bad luck.
23. Bury a woman all in black, and she will return to haunt the family.
24. If rain falls on a corpse, the deceased will go to heaven.
25. If you hear a clap of thunder following a burial, it indicates that the soul of the dead person has reached heaven.

5

COFFINS AND
HEARSES

Six feet of earth make all men of one size.
—*Old Proverb*

One frosty morning a youngster bursting with self-importance knocked at the door of the village carpenter, or cabinetmaker, who in this small community served his neighbors by making almost everything that could be made of wood.

"Aunt Jerushy has had another of her bad spells, and this time she hasn't come out of it. We think she's dead. Grandpa's bringing her down on the sled so's you can fit her to a box. The funeral's at four o'clock this afternoon." His message delivered, the boy turned tail and ran home in hopes of a new assignment.

George, the carpenter, got down some of the pine boards he had smoothed off and placed on a rack in the back room so as to have them ready, and sorted out several. Before the days of embalming, coffins had to be made in a day, and a woodworker usually had some planks dried and ready for his next hurry-up job. Often he—or a friend or member of the family—had to work through the night by candlelight or lamplight in order to finish a coffin quickly.

Jerushy's father arrived with her body, which was carefully measured and taken out back to the cool pantry. George got to work and put together a sturdy "cellar-door," or six-sided coffin and lid. He pulled down a bolt of muslin, measured off some at arm's length from his nose, and tacked a piece inside for lining.

A little after noon George's wife hurried in. She stood at the door. "I was just in the pantry, and, George, I think Jerushy's comin' t' life. The color's back in her cheeks!"

"Color or no color, she's goin' in this box right now," said George angrily. "The funeral's all set for four o'clock and I don't calc'late t' lose my five dollars."

The price of the coffin helps to place this story at about mid-nineteenth century. An 1831 cabinetmaker's price list from the District of Columbia gives us an idea of the charges then for coffins of different woods and different sizes. The "Extras" at the bottom of the list suggest ways to dress up a simple coffin.

2′6″ — poplar	$1.00
3′6″ — poplar	1.25
2′6″ — mahogany	1.25
3′6″ — mahogany	1.50
4′6″ — poplar	1.50
4′6″ — mahogany	1.75
5′ — poplar	2.00
5′ — mahogany	2.50
All above 5′ poplar	2.25
All above 5′ mahogany	3.00
Extra:	
Polished with hard wax	.50
If top is hinged	.50
Putting on breast plate	.12½
Lining with flannel	.31¼
Trimming with lace	.37½
Covering with cloth	1.00

COFFINS AND HEARSES

Our earliest American ancestors were buried without coffins; they were wrapped in shrouds made from cerecloth (linen dipped in wax) or wool, soaked when possible in alum or pitch. On rare occasions a fine shroud was sewn from cashmere. All were rectangular with drawstrings at the top. Very early, though, wood was used to fashion crude coffins. The term "casket" came to be used in the second half of the nineteenth century, after William Smith of Meriden, Connecticut, first made rectangular burial boxes with perpendicular sides.

Frequently, as happened to Jerushy, the corpses was carried by one means or another to the cabinetmaker. Sometimes, however, careful measurements were taken and recorded on a measuring stick, which was taken to the woodshop. The stick was cut exactly the length of the body, and other measurements were carefully written on it. A five-foot, six-inch stick which read "Jerry Kauffman wife July 20, 1880 10 23 7½ 13 plenty high 12 will do" tells us when Jerry's wife died, that the coffin should be a bit longer than five feet, six inches, that head clearance across should be ten inches, widening to twenty-three inches at the shoulders, tapering to seven and a half inches at the foot, and that a depth of a foot would be sufficient. Such sticks were used by the Miller family, cabinet and casket makers of Deer Creek in Washington Township, Johnson County, Iowa. One of the family told about a rider who hustled in to order a coffin only to discover to his dismay that his mule had chewed inches off his measuring stick!

Jacob Miller started his business in about 1850 in the community just west of Iowa City. His first coffins sold for eleven dollars, and were made of walnut or cherry lined with muslin; there was no padding. The coffins had no handles, and were carried on a frame of wooden bars. Usually the coffin was fitted into a "rough box" of one-inch lumber. Church trustees at Lower Deer Creek Cemetery were upset to hear that one Miller customer had ordered a coffin with a rough box "lined with tin to keep

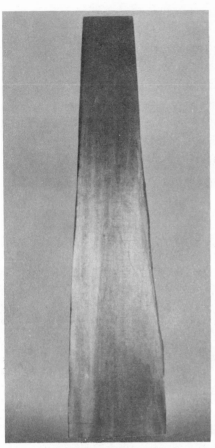

Cooling board upon which corpse was laid out.
Courtesy Hancock Shaker Village, Hancock, Mass.

Early common coffin with plain board lid.
Courtesy Old Museum Village, Monroe, N.Y.

out groundhogs." They hurried to hire a local woodsman, Barney Whetstine, to trap or shoot all the varmints.

Jake Miller made over three hundred coffins, frequently for the neighboring Amish of Sharon Center and Kalona who, well into this century, showed a preference for the old type of coffin rather than the new ready-made affairs.

Traditionally, old-time carpenters brushed together all of the sawdust and shavings accumulated from making a coffin and placed these scraps inside it. Superstition taught that if these bits

of leftover wood were tracked into a house or carelessly shaken
from clothing, they would endanger whomever they touched,
and that person might become death's next victim.

The ordinary pine or poplar coffin was often covered with
alpaca. Pennsylvanians seemed to prefer walnut to other woods,
and this was usually varnished. When cherry was used, beeswax
was apt to be rubbed on and polished with a smoothing iron.
Some softwood boxes were painted. An old-timer was queried
about this:

Wooden coffin with screw-
down lid and glass window.
*Courtesy New York State
Historical Association,
Cooperstown.*

The old red paint? Gosh, the kind they put on cheers and coffins and light stands? That was the plain yellow ochre got out of the ochre pits and roasted or burned into a soft clinker. Same as they get darker ends on the bench bricks 'cause they're laid nearest the fire, you get red instead of yellow ochre after this extry roasting. Then they ground it up. 'Twas awful cheap so they used it on most everything. I seem to have forgot but I reckon this was the old Venetian Red that folks bought for two cents a pound and mixed with oil or milk. Those that lived down Maine way and was handy to fish, used fish oil to stir it up with, and it kept the powder from flying off. Yes, they was uncommon generous with that old paint.

Coffins might have one- or two-piece tops. Some were made so that the lid would slide open a couple of feet for viewing.

Country stores stocked coffin hardware: heavy screws with heads decorated with such things as weeping cypress trees and garlands, long steel tacks, nails shaped like crosses, sets of handles, and inscribed metal plates of brass, copper, tin, and silver. The latter might bear the insignia of fraternal orders or simply say "Our Babe," "Mother," or be inscribed with the name of the deceased.

Lancaster undertaker Abner Eyde commented:

I've made a casket or two in my time but at first it was mostly my job to trim them. We bought the linings by the bolt, and I'd take a good chew of tobacco, a mouthful of tacks and start swinging that hammer. Finished up the job in jig time. Boy have caskets changed during the years! Come lined and ready to bury.

The pall was the cloth laid over the coffin. In most instances it was black, frequently fringed. A white pall was used for children and for women who had died in childbirth. One used by Pennsylvania Moravians in 1844 was described as white with an inscription embroidered in blue: "Jesus My Redeemer Liveth." Palls were owned by churches and stored in the church vestibule with the bier upon which the coffin was set. In early times there were regular bearers and pallbearers, or "upper" and "lower" bearers. The latter carried the coffin; the former lifted the pall so that the bearers were not covered by it.

Some ready-made coffins appeared at about the time of the War of 1812. Among the early ready-mades were some lined with lead. The naval hero John Paul Jones was buried after his death in Paris in 1792 in a lead-lined coffin, his arms and legs wrapped in tinfoil. In 1905 a search was made for his body, and it was recovered, still recognizable.

Coffins have been made from almost every material imaginable, and patents have been applied for and granted for strange materials never actually used commercially and for weird apparatus that never caught on. In 1835 the firm of John White & Associates of Salina, New York, was granted patents to make caskets of stone, marble, and poured cement. In 1836 a patent to manufacture metallic coffins was awarded to James A. Gray of Richmond, Virginia.

Since the first human burial there has been concern over being buried alive. Stories throughout American and earlier history have kept this fear alive. A traveler on Edisto Island, South Carolina, told of seeing a girl of eight or nine standing in the door of a mausoleum:

> She was wearing what looked like an old-fashioned party dress that reached halfway between her knees and ankles.
>
> Her hair was blonde and cut straight, and it was tied in back with a ribbon. And she had a ribbon around her waist and wore ballerina pumps.
>
> I assumed she was crying because she had gotten lost, so I held out my hand and walked slowly toward her. But when I got within a few yards, she vanished

. . . slowly drifting away into oblivion. Her outline
got fainter and fainter until she was gone, leaving me
standing there alone. I was scared to death and wanted
to run—but my legs wouldn't move. Finally, I got
to my car and drove away.

Inquiry disclosed that in the 1850's a young visitor to the island
had died of diphtheria. Fear that the disease might spread caused
a local family named Le Gare to suggest that the child be interred
in their vault, which was done quickly. A Le Gare son died
during the Civil War, and when the tomb was opened to admit
his body, a tiny skeleton was found on the floor just behind the
door. Townspeople claimed that from that time on the door to
the tomb would not stay closed, even after it had been chained;
then the hinges were pulled apart.

As a result of supposedly true stories like this one and the
fiction of writers like Edgar Allan Poe, who was popular in
the mid-nineteenth century, various bizarre systems were invented to prevent accidental burial of the living. In 1843 Christian Eisenbrandt of Baltimore claimed the invention of a
"life-preserving coffin in case of doubtful death." Advertised as
"a new and useful improvement on coffins," it was equipped with
an arrangement of wires and pins, which allowed a spring lid
to fly open if there should be any movement within the box.
A casket with a similar purpose had a flag that unfurled above
ground in case of movement below. Another inventor provided
bells, others, electrical alarms.

One way to identify the dead from the living was supplied by
this old wives' formula:

Touch the flame of a candle to the tip of one of
the great toes of the supposed corpse. A blister will
raise. If life is gone, the blister will be full of air and
will burst noisily when the flame is applied a few
seconds more. If there is still life, the blister will not
burst.

COFFINS AND HEARSES

To discourage tampering with a burial site, whether with the intention of removing the body or stealing valuables interred with the corpse, one applicant for a patent presented a "torpedo coffin"; disturbance of the casket set off an explosive charge! A simpler and less expensive way was to scatter ashes on top of the site, a method employed when grave snatching was common (to show footprints).

Over 125 years ago famous people were doing commercials! Henry Clay, Thomas Jefferson, and Daniel Webster were among others who endorsed the Fiske Metallic Burial Case:

> Gentlemen:
> We witnessed the utility of your ornamental Patent Metallic Burial Case used to convey the remains of the late Hon. John C. Calhoun to the Congressional Cemetery. It impressed us with the belief that it is the best article known to us for transporting the dead to their final resting place.

This casket was cast in the shape of a man lying on his back with his hands folded across his chest. A glass window made the face visible.

By 1860 new materials were being used in experimental coffins, and patents had been issued for coffins made of iron, potter's clay, zinc, and glass.

In 1877 Cruciform Coffins were manufactured in Oswego, New York, and advertised as "the common sense coffin." As suggested by the name, the coffin shape was that of a cross.

John Homrighous of Royalton, Ohio, must have thought that his idea would solve most of the problems of undertakers in the future; his patent of 1878 was for a casket adjustable in size.

By 1900 additional patents had been granted for burial boxes made of vulcanized rubber, aluminum, and papier-mâché.

However, during a time of emergency, such as the flu epidemic of 1918, the substance used to make a coffin became immaterial.

Cast iron coffin with glass window.
Courtesy Old Museum Village, Monroe, N.Y.

No one could provide enough coffins of any material to bury the dead. Undertakers considered themselves lucky to have rough boxes to use. After Pennsylvania's Conemaugh River rose and the dam burst, causing the Johnstown flood, even floating debris was pulled from the retreating waters to make crude boxes for burials.

A "preserver" or "corpse cooler" was in common use in the last half of the 1800's. One I have seen was wooden, paint-grained, with a galvanized liner. Ice was packed around the liner, which extended over the shoulders. A shield at the shoulders retained the ice, and a glass window made the face visible. There were openings to allow replenishing of the ice, and a hose drained

Two later wooden coffins. Tops will open for "viewing."
Courtesy Claude A. Lipe Funeral Home, Northville, N.Y.

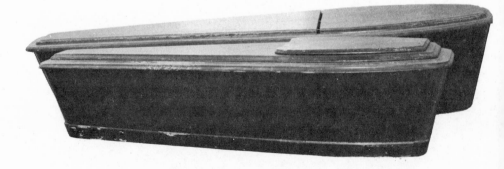

water into a bucket beneath the cooler. Before the time of the cooler, bodies were sometimes laid on sod to keep them cool.

Excerpts from the daybooks of David Evans, a Philadelphia cabinetmaker from 1774 to 1811, frequently mention details about his manufacture of coffins:

1788: Aug. 12   Made a coffin for Wm. Churchill Houston Esq. of Trenton, who died at Geiss's Tavern on Frankfort Road.

Sept. 1   Estate James Allen, to making a Mahogany Coffin for the deceased, with inscription plate and handles; ordered by his grandfather Thomas Lawrence Esq., £8.

Oct. 15   Estate John Lukens (Surveyor General) making a Mahogany Coffin and handles for deceased £8.10.
N.B. This coffin was 2'3" over the shoulders.

Nov. 26   This morning a fire broke out next door to the Bunch of Grapes, in Third St. near Arch—consumed the house in which were eight persons, five of whom got out, and three, the widow Preston and her two sons were burned before assistance could be given. Making a coffin for the three remains found in ruins £1.17.6, abated 15/.

1792: Nov. 6   Estate Thomas Riche, Lacing in best manner, full trim'd, with inscription plate, Cherrubs &c. for coffin of deceased, £4.

Nov. 20   Mr. Randolph, Attorney General U.S. making a coffin for his black servant, £2.5.

Dec. 26   Stephen Page, Mahogany Coffin, Inscription plate, Flower-pots, handles, for his wife, £8.10.

1793: Mar. 7   Daniel Rundle, making a Coffin for his wife Ann Rundle, covered with Black

Cloth, lined with White Flannel, Inscription Plate, Flowerpots and Cherrubs, Handles, and full laced, £15.

Sept. 11   Estate of my brother Richard Gardner, a Walnut Coffin, £3. He died of Yellow Fever. Was a Clerk in the Bank of Pennsylvania and an admirable accountant. Buried in Friends' Ground.

1797: July 14   Estate Caleb Emlen—making the deceased a Mahogany Coffin with silver handles. £8.10.

Evans was one of Philadelphia's leading cabinetmakers and a prominent citizen, as we can guess from his customers. The furniture he made was of high quality, the repair work reliable. He mentions making a Pembroke table, repairing a mahogany dining table for Vice President John Adams, making a reading desk for Congress and a mahogany clock case for the University of Pennsylvania, and shipping on the sloop *Highland* 16 Venetian blinds for the War Office, Washington, D. C. His business seems to have been improved rather than damaged by the war. His records show items such as 161 sets of tent poles for the United States of America, 4 camp chairs for Captain Francis Wade, a box for camp equipage for Lieutenant Fred Hoysted. Evans became prosperous but remained sympathetic to those who weren't. People were not required to pay full price if they were in "low circumstances." A local chimney sweep was allowed to clean Evans' chimney in exchange for a coffin for his wife.

The most elaborate coffins I have heard of were ordered by Dr. Henry Hiller and his wife. The doctor arrived in this country from Germany in 1873 to live in Wilmington, Massachusetts, and he maintained an office in Boston from which he sold his patent medicine, an elixir "good for anything that ailed man or beast." Sales were tremendous, and Dr. Hiller became wealthy.

A Cambridge cabinetmaker, James MacGregor, was asked to start work on two magnificent caskets, which the doctor and his wife sketched for him. MacGregor estimated that it would take him, even with four assistants, about seven years to complete the assignment. It was agreed that he would be paid forty dollars a week, and the project was started. Each coffin was to be made of mahogany four inches thick. Fanciful carvings were to be cut into the wood. Two ivy vines were to run around the edge of the box, meeting where a skull had been carved. Angels, cupids, and dragons by the dozens were to be carved along the sides. Bats were to fly above the heads of serpents; a big owl was to hold a tiny mouse in its claws.

Inside each coffin eight lion's paws of brass, weighing 475 pounds, were used to support a steel hammock suspended from above. (The whole affair eventually rose five feet off the floor.) On each casket's cover there were to be gold and silver plates holding portraits of Hiller and his wife and their twenty-three children—including seven sets of twins—all of whom had died in infancy.

Dr. Hiller died on November 7, 1888, before his coffin was completed, so his body was placed in a vault. About a year later the coffin was finished; its cost had reached thirty thousand dollars. The funeral was planned. A special train brought mourners out from Boston to Wilmington, where even the town hall was draped and a large crayon portrait was hung to honor the city's adopted son. The funeral procession started at the Hiller home, as a military band played dirges and two thousand people bearing lighted torches followed afoot. The walkers were followed to Wildwood Cemetery by carryalls, hayracks, buck- boards, and hundreds of bicycles.

When, three and a half years after Henry Hiller was buried, his wife's coffin was completed, it was delivered and set up in the parlor! At first she delighted in climbing up into it to show her friends how she would look in her magnificent final resting place. Later she had a wax model of herself made and dressed in exquisite funeral robes that cost twenty thousand dollars. These were created from five hundred yards of lace handmade in

France; five thousand daisies had been embroidered on the lace.

Funeral preparations and expenses ate into the Hiller fortune until Mrs. Hiller decided to capitalize on the whole affair. She hired Boston's Horticultural Hall and had eight truck horses transport her casket there. Ten policemen dressed in mourning guarded the exhibit with billy clubs covered with black velvet. Curious Bostonians and their visitors paid a fee, then circled the unique burial box with its wax figure.

Mrs. Henry Hiller enjoyed being Mrs. Henry Hiller. When in 1893 she married Peter Surrette, her coachman, she had his name legally changed to Henry Hiller.

At Mrs. Hiller's funeral it took ten men to lift the coffin, which broke the porch railing and almost upset the extra-sturdy hearse that had been provided to carry it. Four black horses draped with black netting pulled the coffin on its bier. This was followed by an open landau filled with flowers, then ten hacks appropriately draped and pulled by black horses. There was a long procession, and crowds overran both the church and the cemetery. Certainly the two funerals lived up to the Hillers' proudest anticipations.

John Bowman, owner of a thriving tannery, also made expansive plans to honor his family. He concentrated, not on coffins, but on a handsome mausoleum in Cuttingsville, Vermont. Bowman had lived for years in upper New York State with his wife, Jennie. They had two children: Addie, who died when she was four months old, and Ella. Despite the early death of Addie, the Bowmans lived happily, finally making plans to return to John's native Vermont, for which he longed. He and Jennie planned to build an elaborate mansion there, but the illness and death of both Jennie and Ella put an end to that hope.

Heartbroken, John went back to Vermont alone and settled in Cuttingsville. He donated land for a cemetery next to the Community Church and obtained the town's permission for a large Grecian mausoleum, which he planned to construct at the cemetery's entrance, inscribed "Laurel Glen Mausoleum, Sacred to the

Bowman mausoleum, Cuttingsville, Vt., with larger-than-life statue
of John Bowman on steps.

Memory of a Sainted Wife and Daughters." Building began in
July 1880, and 125 workmen and artisans, all of them expert
in their particular fields, worked for a year, using seven hundred
tons of granite, fifty tons of marble, twenty thousand bricks,
525 barrels of cement, ten barrels of plaster, and one hundred
loads of sand. The project cost Mr. Bowman seventy-five thousand dollars.

The tomb is made of white marble with broad steps leading
to a gate. Most impressive of all is a larger-than-life statue of
Bowman himself, waiting on the steps holding his mourning
cloak, tall silk hat, gloves, and a delicate wreath. His right hand
holds a key to the tomb. This lifelike piece of sculpture was
done by an Italian sculptor named Turini, whose signature appears at Bowman's feet. Inside the gate are busts of each member
of the family, with plate-glass mirrors arranged to create an
optical illusion of depth.

Bowman built a mansion across from Laurel Glen. It has been
said that he became obsessed with thoughts of reincarnation and
believed that someday his women would return to him. For

ten years he spent an hour or more each evening at the tomb, quietly meditating or trying to find solace in reading the Bible. In 1891 Bowman died and was laid to rest beside his beloved family.

He left a trust fund of fifty thousand dollars to maintain the tomb and the residence. Among instructions to the servants, he asked that the dining table be set for dinner each evening. In 1953 Bowman's estate was so depleted that furniture from the residence had to be sold to maintain the grounds. Eventually the house went too, but the mausoleum stands as sturdy as when Bowman was alive, perpetuating his pride in his family, and perhaps in himself.

"Mad Jack" Percival, captain of "Old Ironsides," the frigate *Constitution*, bought some fine mahogany planks when the ship was anchored in the harbor of Madagascar. He had the ship's carpenter measure him and construct an elegant coffin. It was beautifully carved and laboriously polished, then set up in the Captain's cabin.

The *Constitution* weathered numerous storms, and during especially heavy weather, the cabin boy is reputed to have cried, "We're sinking! We're sinking! We'll all be in Heaven before morning."

Captain Percival replied, "That's all right with me. I've got more friends on the other side than on this. However, I'm not climbing into that box just yet."

Ship, captain, and crew withstood the storm, and the captain, in time, retired to Dorchester, Massachusetts. He never did use the coffin from Madagascar. For years it sat in his front yard filled with water for all of the dogs and horses that happened to be thirsty while going down Percival Street. "Old Ironsides" is still on display in Boston Harbor, but Mad Jack's coffin no longer exists.

Occasionally a cabinetmaker or an undertaker met an especially complicated burial. This was the case when Angus

Simple Shaker hearse, with bier. Painted blue.
Courtesy Hancock Shaker Village, Hancock, Mass.

McAskill, the Cape Breton giant, died in Englishtown, Nova Scotia. The Halifax *Acadian Recorder* described him as "the well-known giant . . . by far the tallest man in Nova Scotia, perhaps in British America . . . his mild and gentle manner endeared him to all who had the pleasure of his acquaintance." McAskill was seven feet, nine inches tall, weighed 425 pounds, had shoulders forty-four inches wide, hands eight inches wide and a foot long. Two carpenters worked six hours to make his eight-foot coffin, which was constructed of pine and lined with white cloth.

The following anecdote about a cabinetmaker was told to me as true. The winter was at its stormiest when an elderly lady died back in the country near Lewey Lake in the Adirondacks. Her body was fastened on a hand sleigh and drawn down to Speculator, where the nearest carpenter lived. While the corpse lay in the back room, the carpenter worked at making her a pine box. When it was completed, he attempted to lay the body in the coffin. It wouldn't fit. Through miscalculation the coffin was too short. The workman surveyed his startling discovery for a few moments and made his decision. The funeral was set, the coffin was needed, so he reached for his saw and shortened the legs of the cadaver. He placed the feet inside the box, screwed the lid down tight, and delivered the coffin. Later the man explained his action. "She was always a thrifty one. Certainly she wouldn't uv wanted me t' put the family t' any extry expense."

In our earliest days neighbors carried a body to its final resting place on a frame of planks. Later an open wagon or sleigh pulled by a single horse served as a hearse. Diarist Samuel Sewell reported the 1697 funeral of Colonel Shrimpton: "Ten companies. No Herse nor Trumpet, but a horse led. Mourning coach also & Horses in Mourning, Scutcheons on their sides and Death's Heads on their Foreheads."

In 1798 when Joshua Brown, a Pennsylvanian of Quaker persuasion, died in the township of Little Britain, his sons carried him from his house in a plain coffin, which was tied to a four-wheeled chassis topped by a wide board. The undertaker rode ahead with the body to Penn Hill Meeting House while mourners followed.

The first hearses were like that used for Joshua Brown, merely biers on large wheels. In the country open wagons were filled with straw to cushion the coffin. Waterproof covers were kept on hand in case of inclement weather. The early covered, horse-drawn hearses appear fragile to us today, the chassis teetering on high springs and spindly wheels. Some were about the size of the old tin-peddler's cart, with a door at the back and only one compartment. There was a roller on the rear floor to ease the coffin in and out, and open windows on the sides, often three. The first hearses had no glass in the windows. Some had woolen draperies or fringed curtains with tassels. Although the chassis of these early vehicles were plain, there were apt to be orna-

Early hearse. Notice the carved wooden torches, draped, which ornament the top. Fringed and tasseled shades are typical.

Courtesy Old Museum Village, Monroe, N.Y.

ments on the top, a series of urns or draped torches with eternal
wooden flames. The driver sat on a box attached to the front
with no roof overhead. Hearses for adults were painted black.
Small-sized ones for infants and children were often white.

Later special carriages were constructed with wide and comfortable high seats for top-hatted drivers, and these vehicles
became more and more elaborate until in the late nineteenth
century their size and decoration rivaled that of contemporary
circus wagons only slightly subdued. They had fancy carving
along the lines of construction, which was often gilded. Heavy
plate glass with beveled edges covered the windows, and the
hangings were shirred and draped and ornamented with long
tassels. The interiors were carefully finished. In the winter
bobsleds replaced wheels, a practice more common in rural areas
than in cities.

This hearse (1865), considered very elegant in its time, has black plumes and black upholstery trimmed with silver.

Note the curved glass at the front and rear of this circular hearse (1870), which is all black.

One horse pulled the early lightweight "dead wagons," but two were necessary for the later heavier vehicles. Before the days of undertaking establishments, churches owned the hearses, which were rented out by the sexton. Livery stables, too, provided hearses as well as horses. Eli B. Prowl, who took over his father's stable at 14 East Walnut Street in Lancaster, Pennsylvania, in 1884, offered thirty rigs, fifteen hacks, and three hearses. His sixty-by-ninety-six-foot stable was three stories high and equipped with an electric elevator.

Black horses were kept especially for funerals, along with heavy veils of net with which the horses were draped.

Hearse on runners for winter use, circa 1875. Chassis was placed on wheels in summer.

Courtesy Old Museum Village, Monroe, N.Y.

Ornate "circus wagon" hearse, late 1800's.

Courtesy Old Museum Village, Monroe, N.Y.

Lincoln's funeral train, drawn by the engine *Nashville*, traveled nearly two thousand miles in twelve days.

In the cities funeral trolley cars came to be used. These cars, which carried coffin, flowers, and mourners together, followed regular routes to the most popular cemeteries.

In rural Amish communities the *todtenwagen*, a spring wagon that resembled a large Amish carriage, continued to be used until the present century.

Hearse built by Charles L. Kenyon, undertaker and cabinetmaker of Elkland, Pa., 1889.
Photo by Pennsylvania Historical and Museum Commission, Harrisburg.

COFFINS AND HEARSES

Soon after the beginning of the twentieth century, however, auto hearses came into use almost everywhere. Abner Eyde describes this period.:

> The boss contacted the Welsh-Detroit people about a chassis and instead of having a touring car put on top of it he ordered a hearse. He always was ahead of his time. He had special seats made for his family to take a ride on Sundays. That hearse was used for a wagon to carry rough boxes and for funerals and everything else. We kept gasoline in a large tank with a spigot. It was poured from a smaller can into the auto tank through a funnel covered with a chamois. That took out the impurities.
>
> In time we had mixed funerals, one or two motor cars and the rest buggies. That sure was hard on the machines. We never forgot to carry the repair kits for tires. Often we had to stop and use them during a funeral procession.
>
> When F. F. bought the Maxwell touring car about 1910 it was a real curiosity around town. You didn't take a drivers' test in those days. I'd taught myself to drive when we got the hearse and when we hired another embalmer, Ross Eyler, he just sat beside me once or twice to learn.

Child's hearse with coffin, circa 1900. Such vehicles for children were usually white, yellow, or occasionally, blue.
Photo by Pennsylvania Historical and Museum Commission, Harrisburg.

You just up and wrote to Harrisburg for your license. I think it cost two dollars. It was a metal badge and said "Licensed Driver" on it. You pinned it on the lapel of your coat, or, since it was the style to wear gauntlet gloves, most drivers pinned it on one of their long cuffs.

Those first unreliable gasoline-powered hearses must have provided unexpected excitement when they frightened the horses they met or broke down at inconvenient times. Nevertheless, the day of the peaceful procession, led by carefully disciplined horses pulling an open wagon with its cellar-door coffin cushioned on a bed of straw, was over.

6

PLACES OF BURIAL

'Twas an awful yet pleasing Treat . . .
—*Samuel Sewell upon visit to cemetery*

Near the village of Sapinta in northeastern Romania, there is a charming place known as the Merry Cemetery. Stan Ion Petras, a wood carver, is responsible for the brightly painted markers that have made the cemetery famous. The remarkable thing about Petras' work is that his markers are people in bas-relief going about their daily routine—milking goats, spinning, dancing to a fiddle tune, chopping wood, picking apples, tending beehives. A verse is found on each marker, really a "biography in little," as someone once aptly defined an epitaph, but in translation the rhymes are lost:

> Green leaves of Cornel
> My name is Elie Petrinjel.
> I was my village's oldest man;
> There was no better dancer . . .
> I danced to many tunes,
> In Baie Mare and in Bucharest, too.
> May all who look at me,

DEATH IN EARLY AMERICA

Dance as I did.
I hope you will live
To reach my age, 96 years.

Petras made his first unique marker in 1935, and has been filling orders ever since. He is the carver, the painter, and the poet in the creation of these imaginative grave "stones." He demands from his clients only the freedom to show the dead as he knew them: the nurse, the apple picker, the dancing ancient.

Unlike many sleepy and peaceful American cemeteries, the Merry Cemetery bustles with the tasks of a village, suggesting, as author Donald Stoddard says, that "the dead live on through their work, their accomplishments. . . . The cemetery smacks of vitality and the joy of men's 'doings.'" Here is a place for the dead that is a joy for the living.

Marbletown, the boneyard, Boot Hill, Potter's Field, *Gottes Acker*—all of these refer to burying grounds. Over the years

Burying ground at Ephrata Cloisters, Ephrata, Pa.

What remains of a single-family farm cemetery on the property of Arleigh Lee, Fishhouse Road, near Lake Sacandaga, N.Y.

American cemeteries have run a gamut of change. In the earliest days of colonial settlement, burial places were often camouflaged in hopes that savages might not count the number dead. In Puritan times the churchyard cemetery became a place to wander or picnic in between church services, reading warnings to the living along with eulogies to the dead. Gracious symbols of heavenly promise mingled with horrid reminders of man's vulnerability. Later, elaborate family tombs held stacks of coffins. In the country private family burying places, usually atop a hill in rocky ground unfit for cultivation, appeared on almost every farm. One wonders why there aren't more burials on private property today. In New York State, for instance, few restrictions exist: a family burying ground may be no longer than three acres and no closer to a residence than one hundred feet without permission of the owner. N. P. Willis, traveling across New York State in the mid-1800's and commenting on family cemeteries, wondered why there were so many then:

> All through this region, and towards Otsego Lake, as well as through the valley of the Kobleskill, I ob-

served that every farm had its grave; and this, not fenced in or secluded, but with the white slab rising from the middle of a crop of grain, or a field of potatoes. Among such prosperous people, this can not be from any economy of hearse or church-yard; and, as a man can not very well see his barns and cattle from underground, nor, by force of vicinage, rise again with the crops sown around him, I do not very well understand how the custom could become so general.

Villages became cities, and when churchyard burial grounds became crowded, large tracts were set aside outside the cities. Before cemeteries in the suburbs became customary, the older dead were sometimes disinterred to make room for their descendants. For a time, after the graveyard of a Lancaster, Pennsylvania, Methodist Church became filled, an additional three feet of earth was dumped on top of the graves and the sites resold. Eventually, though, the town authorities made this solution to the problem illegal.

During the days of the Victorians, the more elaborate cemeteries became popular spots for Sunday outings. Today in many communities the burying ground has become a "Memory Garden," where there are only tiny markers. The grounds in these cemeteries are carefully manicured, and soft music whispers from hidden speakers, but we have forgotten the tradition of burying the dead with the feet toward the east so that on Resurrection Morn the immortal rises facing the sun.

The eminent judge and diarist Samuel Sewell describes briefly his visit to the family tomb:

> Dec. 25, 1696—'Twas wholly dry, and I went at noon to see what order things were set; and there I was entertained with a view of, and converse with, the Coffins of my dear Father Hull, Mother Hull, Cousin Quinsey, and my Six Children. . . . 'Twas an awful yet pleasing Treat.

A problem connected with family-size underground tombs was sealing them against water. Church sextons much preferred individual interments. One commented: "When a tomb is opened for a new interment, dilapidated coffins are often found lying about, and bones, and mud and water on the bottom."

During the colonial times of Sewell, when the cities along the East Coast of the country had become more populated and stone-and-brick churches, many patterned after cathedrals in Europe, had raised their spires, burial *under* churches, in European tradition, was also practiced. It was even possible, for an extra fee, for a church member to be buried under the very pew in which he had sat when alive. L. M. Sargent, the sexton of a Boston church during the early nineteenth century, tells of sneaking down as a child to watch an under-church interment. This occurred in 1796.

> The body was carried into a dimly-lighted vault. I was so small and short, that I could see scarcely anything. But the deep sepulchral voice of Mr. Parker . . . filled me with most delightful horror. I listened and shivered. At length he uttered the words "earth to earth" and Grossman, who did his duty marvellously well when he was sober, rattled on the coffin a whole shovelful of coarse gravel—"ashes to ashes"—another shovelful of gravel—"dust to dust"—another: it seemed as if shovel and all were cast upon the coffin lid. I never forgot it.

Preachers themselves earned a place of honor, and they were interred right in front of the pulpit.

Frequently, in areas populated by the Dutch, at least, it was the schoolmaster who earned an extra pittance for digging a grave beneath the floor of the church and carefully removing all of the dirt from the premises. In the Dutch settlement Flatbush, the burial beneath the church itself cost two pounds for a child under six, three pounds for a person from six to sixteen, and four pounds for an adult. Today, in Quincy, Massachusetts, President

John Adams lies next to his Abigail, beneath the Congregational Church.

The epitaph of a doctor labeled "a French physician" was published in a Boston newspaper. I could not discover whether he lived and died here or in his native France, or whether he merely provided a nom de plume for a propagandist.

Epitaph on a Celebrated French Physician

Here lies,
Under the pure and breezy skies,
The dust
Of Simon Peter, the devout and just,
Doctor of Medicine,
At his request,
He sleeps in the Earth's sweet wholesome breast,
Rather than in a noisy cemetery
Under a church, where all the great they bury,
It were, he said, a sin
Past all enduring,
A sin, which to commit he was unwilling;
Should he, who, while alive, got fame and bread,
The sick by curing,
Entirely change his hand and go, when dead,
The well to killing?

Controversy over burial under churches raged. A writer for the *Cincinnati Miscellany* commented:

> Before the establishment of Rural Cemeteries near the Eastern Cities, the custom prevailed of burying the dead under the churches. They were crowded in so revolting a manner as to render the air in churches unwholesome . . . finally the custom was prohibited, and cemeteries were established a few miles out, in all Atlantic cities.

Doctors too, were vehement in their criticisms. Buchan states in about 1850:

PLACES OF BURIAL

In great cities, so many things tend to contaminate the air, that it is no wonder it proves to be so fatal to the inhabitants. . . . It is very common in this country to have churchyards in the middle of populous cities. Certain it is that thousands of putrid carcasses, so near the surface of the earth in a place where the air is confined, can not fail to taint it; and that such air, when breathed into the lungs must occasion diseases.

Burying within churches is a practice still more detestable. Churches . . . are seldom open above once a week, are never ventilated by fires nor open windows, and rarely kept clean. This occasions that damp, musty, unwholesome smell . . . and renders it a very unsafe place for the living.

It was difficult to find an approved final resting place for some: the criminal, the suicide, the stranger, the illegitimate. A burial ground for the town's indigent and friendless was called Potter's Field. Sometimes this adjoined a regular cemetery; sometimes it was isolated on the outskirts of town. In Lancaster, Pennsylvania, it was 1798 before an illegitimate child could be buried in the yard

It was difficult to find a burial place for the criminal, the suicide, the illegitimate.
Courtesy Old Fort Museum, Schoharie, N.Y.

of the First Reformed Church. Even then the bell could not be tolled, and the church's pastor was not allowed to take part in, or even attend, any sort of ceremony. By 1823 the consistory of this church resolved that "persons who live in open lusts and died without repentance" should not be allowed any tolling of the bells or a minister, but they could be buried in an obscure rear section of the burying grounds. Toward the end of the nineteenth century, Ab Eyde commented on a double hanging that took place in Lancaster, and reported that the criminals were buried in St. Anthony's, in unblessed ground, and that "practically all hangings were buried there."

Nathan Orlando Greenfield, hanged in 1877, at Onondaga Penitentiary in Syracuse, New York, for the murder of his wife, Alice, was the last person to suffer such a fate in New York State. His parents chose to bury Nathan on the home farm in upper New York in an unmarked grave. For many months, however, they hung a lantern over this site and lighted it every evening to discourage curiosity seekers and body snatchers.

The disposal of the body of a suicide used to be a real problem. Ordinarily the suicide could not be buried in ground blessed by the church. And people were superstitious, too, about suicide. For example, Allen Ketlaw was a strange man who was not popular with his neighbors. They said he possessed an "uncanny" sense, which made them uncomfortable with him. When Ketlaw shot himself with his own musket, his body lay in a rough box for five days while townspeople argued about it; no one wanted the body on his property. Finally one farmer relented and gave permission for burial on his land within his woods. Scores of people watched as a shallow grave was dug beneath tall trees. The weather was wild and windy, perfect for the final commitment of Ketlaw's unwanted remains to the ground. The pine box was brought over the fields to the woods in an open wagon. The horse stamped its feet, shook its head nervously, and seemed anxious to be rid of its burden. Finally, as the casket was quietly lowered, a sound whispered through the silence, and the onlookers started in fear. A moaning voice repeated, "Dig it deeper. Dig it deeper. Dig it deeper."

The workmen picked up their shovels, for certainly it seemed like a human voice to those who heard it. However, after their initial shock, members of the crowd looked around and listened intently. They found that the "voice" was really a sound made by twisted elm branches rubbing against each other.

During the second quarter of the 1800's, cemeteries outside of cities became common. The burying grounds resembled, and came to be used like, city parks; shrubs and trees abounded and municipalities boasted of their elegance. Public transportation to them was provided, often in later years by trolley car.

By 1830 Boston, New York, and Philadelphia had already developed cemetery tracts chosen for their accessibility and natural beauty. Laurel Hill, a splendid country estate in Pennsylvania, became Laurel Hill, a beautifully landscaped burying ground, and Philadelphia claimed it would add "the skill of the sculptor, the graceful hand of the florist, the chastened design of the architect, and let the genius and the talent of the land throw around their whole their most exalted strains of poetry and religious feeling."

N. P. Willis described Laurel Hill:

> The cemetery occupies a lofty promontory above the Schuylkill . . . shaded with pines and other ornamental trees of great age and beauty. The views down upon the river, and through the sombre glades and alleys of the burial-grounds, are unsurpassed for sweetness and repose. The elegance, which marks everything Philadelphian, is shown already in the few monuments erected. An imposing gateway leads you in from the high road, and a freestone group, large as life, representing Old Mortality at work on an inscription, and Scott leaning on a tombstone to watch his toil, faces the entrance. I noticed the area of one tomb enclosed by a chain of hearts, cast beautifully in iron. The whole was laid out in gravel-walks, and there was

no grave without its flowers. . . . I look upon this and Mount Auburn at Cambridge, as delightful indications of a purer growth in our national character than politics and money-getting. It is a real-life poetry, which reflects as much glory upon the age as the birth of a Homer.

Stories about haunted cemeteries abound. This one came to me from a folklore student:

This was told to me by my grandmother from Aberdeen, Maryland. She said that when my great-grandfather was about nineteen or twenty, he had a summer job in a lumber camp in the low Pennsylvania mountains. This was about ninety years ago. He went home on Sunday, walked all the way. The road led over a low mountain. Near the top was an old, old, abandoned cemetery. This particular night there was no moon, and the stars gave only a dim light. As Great-Grandpa passed the little cemetery he thought, "Here, if anywhere, there could be ghosts."

So he climbed up on the stone wall surrounding the burying ground and bellowed, "All ye ghosts and goblins, arise!"

A chill went over him. The skin of his scalp began to tingle, for white forms began rising from the tall grass around the tombstones. It was a long, long minute before he realized that he had disturbed a slumbering flock of sheep.

There was a rumor around Milltown in northern Pennsylvania that the local cemetery was haunted. Many folks thought they had proof of this, for they had heard strange, mournful sounds issuing from the cemetery. To hear this sound at night was especially unnerving, and people began to avoid that locale whenever possible. At last a farmer, who would have no truck with ghostly spirits, heard the sound in midday and summoned one of his hired hands. Together they went into the enclosure and looked and listened. Before long their attention was drawn to the split-rail fence on the north side of the grounds, and they realized that the sound became audible as the north wind hit the split rails. The breeze blew through the fence, the sound rising and falling from a whisper to a whistle with the intensity of the wind.

Another old tale, reported in *The American Weekly Mercury* of Newport, Rhode Island, on March 30, 1722, is more difficult to explain. During the winter 1721–1722 a woman of Narragansett died of smallpox. Burial was quick and quiet for epidemics were much feared. Soon after the burial a strange phenomenon started to occur frequently—every evening, according to someone living within sight of the grave. At nine or ten o'clock a small light appeared on or near the grave site. The flicker grew "to great bigness and brightness" until it would resemble a conflagration. Even on a dark night everything could be seen with distinctness: tufts of grass upon the ground, the bark upon the trees. Sparks flew. A person wrapped as if in a winding sheet with arms folded could be seen. The light moved about very quickly over a distance of perhaps half a mile.

This strange occurrence, reported by apparently reputable eyewitnesses, was never explained satisfactorily by people who didn't believe that spirits, even those who leave this universe hurriedly without finishing what they had started, have the power to return to earth with visible manifestations of their presence.

There are several obvious differences between American Moravian cemeteries and run-of-the-mill places of burial in this country. First, Moravian markers are laid flat and they are all the same size to show that, in the eyes of God, all men are equal. The stones are referred to as "breast stones" in contrast to the "head" and "foot" stones usually found in graveyards. The Moravians have no family plots but lay the cemeteries out like graph paper with a marker in each square. The one I visited in Lititz was carefully groomed, and purple violets sprinkled the grass. Each grave marker was numbered, and the burial sites were

Moravian cemetery, Lititz, Pa.

filled in categories as people died: young boys; young girls; the married, by sexes; the unmarried, by sexes. In Lititz married men and women were buried opposite each other. The graves were made with molds in only two sizes—for children and for adults.

Some Shaker cemeteries, including the one at Niskayuna, New York, have markers of the same size, placed equidistant, as neat as the Shakers themselves in their uniform dress. The rows are exact. Even in burying their dead, the Shakers remained precise. Other Shaker communities enclosed the cemeteries and used a

Unusual urn design on stone in Moravian cemetery, Lititz, Pa.

Typical breast stone in Moravian cemetery, Lititz, Pa.

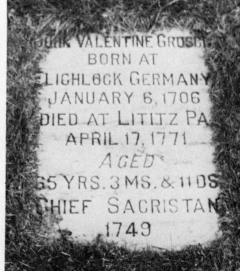

JOHN VALENTINE GROSC
BORN AT
ELIGHLOCK GERMANY
JANUARY 6, 1706
DIED AT LITITZ PA
APRIL 17, 1771
AGED
65 YRS. 3 MS. & 11 DS
CHIEF SACRISTAN
1749

Shaker cemetery for first American colony near Niskayuna, N.Y. Shakers often used only initials on markers.

single monument to commemorate all of the dead buried there. The Hancock Village Cemetery has an iron fence around it and a large single marker in the center.

Church Amish provide burying grounds next to their churches, and these are carefully tended. The House Amish locate their graveyards in the country, in a field or down a winding lane. There are no shrubs or trees; the plots are bare. Sometimes grazing sheep shear the grass. There is no charge for Amish grave sites, and annually the menfolk fill in sunken spots, mow,

Single stone commemorating all of the dead in small, fenced cemetery of Hancock Shakers, Hancock, Mass.

and right tilting stones. It is not the custom of these people to visit their cemeteries frequently.

A number of Americans have had unique funerals and burials according to their own plans: others, due to circumstances they did not foresee. An acquaintance of mine requested that his body be cremated and his ashes mingled with the cold, spring-fed waters of Lake George near his summer home. Another acquaintance was buried at sea, in the very yacht that he had loved and operated for years. These burials, in accordance with the wishes of the deceased, contrast with the burial of a gentleman from Montana named Arnett, who was killed while gambling; he died with one hand gripping his six-shooter, the other, a poker hand. And he was buried that way.

Some had reason enough to suggest special arrangements for their corpses. Valentine Tapley, who died at Spenserburg, Missouri, in 1910, had sworn a half century before that if Abraham Lincoln was elected to the presidency, he, Tapley, would not cut or trim his beard thereafter. He kept his promise, and with the growth of his twelve-and-a-half-foot beard, his fame also grew. While alive, Tapley wound his beard carefully in silk and wore it wrapped around his body. The luxuriant appendage was laundered and groomed with patience, and Valentine's pride in it became so great that the fear of injury to his glorious whiskers became an obsession. Tapley's will provided for the strongest coffin and vault obtainable, and he was buried in a tomb as burglar-proof as it was possible to make it. No grave robbers or pranksters ever cut, trimmed, or so much as stroked the long silky chin whiskers of Val Tapley.

Reuben John Smith of Buffalo, New York, and Amesbury, Massachusetts, was buried sitting in his Morris chair. Reuben John, in life, was a tall, lean gentleman with a flowing moustache. He was a house painter and a shy and pleasant bachelor, who dressed conservatively in dark suits and a black derby. After being poisoned by the lead in the paint he used daily, he changed his occupation to hack driving. Shortly after the Civil War, he moved from Buffalo to Amesbury, where he lived the rest of his life. Smith had two hobbies, playing checkers and visiting the courthouse to observe trials and lawsuits.

Reuben John gave considerable thought to the fact that upon his death there would be no one to take responsibility for his funeral and burial. He figured he should settle these matters himself, ahead of time. On a visit to Patton's Hollow Marble Works in 1888, he talked to Charlie Davis and gave him a sketch of a tomb he wanted in Mount Prospect Cemetery. This, according to Smith's plans, was to be made from the finest Vermont marble and the best Boston brick. There was to be a steel door facing west with *two* keys. The structure would be ten feet six inches by five feet six inches with an elevation of seven feet six inches, and would have a flat, low-pitched roof. There would be seats within the building.

Construction started and Smith visited often to oversee the work. When the tomb was completed, he visited it every weekend, sometimes inviting guests: "Come out and see the view from my coffin next Sunday afternoon." For ten years Smith spent as much time as he could spare at Mount Prospect.

The far-seeing gentleman liked his comfort, and after due meditation visited the funeral parlor he had chosen and spoke to a Mr. Austin about certain details. He wanted to be buried "in a sitting position in a reclining chair"—this is the language of his will—and a Morris chair seemed most appropriate, so with the undertaker's approval, he chose an oak "recliner" beautifully upholstered in russet leather. Smith mentioned that he would expect to be dressed in an overcoat if the day of his funeral proved cold. Austin suggested a hat, and they agreed upon this.

Death did occur on a cold day, January 23, 1899, and the plans of the deceased were followed meticulously. Since everyone had been gossiping about the arrangements, the streets of Amesbury were lined with the curious, but they trickled back home, disappointed. Reuben and his chair were draped with a black shroud when they were carefully transported to the tomb. The undertaker commented, however: "Reuben looked just as natural as life sitting there in his Morris chair just like he was taking his noonday nap."

According to rumor, the deceased had offered a hundred dollars to anyone willing to spend his first night in the tomb with him, but there were no takers. Folks said that several things besides Reuben John and his chair had been placed in the tomb: a favorite checkerboard, a tin box with clippings about his burial, a table, a candle and matches, and, perhaps most important, a key to the heavy steel door.

Lightning hit the tomb in 1930 and completely wrecked it. It was repaired and sealed tight, and remains today covered with cobblestones and surrounded by white birch trees.

The destruction of the tomb is reminiscent of the fate of another sarcophagus, that of famed "Aunt Harriet" Cruger, who lived in a castlelike home near Herkimer, New York. She had a marvelous marble sarcophagus prepared and placed in her cellar, where she wished to be buried, because she had been happy in her castle and wanted to stay there eternally. After her death relatives refused to follow the old lady's wishes, and she was interred in a traditional cemetery. After a bit the young folks had the marble casket hoisted up out of the cellar and, in an attempt to gain some use from it, placed it in the yard and filled it with water for the horses. This arrangement had hardly been completed when a magnificent storm blew up and lightning struck the horse trough, breaking off great chunks and leaving it useless. Aunt Harriet's wrath was far-reaching.

In 1857, at twenty-seven, Nancy Martin died at sea while traveling with her father. He wanted desperately to get her body home for interment. After conferring with the ship's captain, Mr. Martin arranged for his daughter's body to be placed in a cask of alcohol. This was done, and upon arriving in Wilmington, North Carolina, they buried cask and body in that city's Oakdale Cemetery.

PLACES OF BURIAL

An elderly gentleman referred to as Old Peddler Hill who lived near Rochester, New Hampshire, was buried in a lead coffin on Blue Jobe Mountain. The lead box, like Nancy Martin's cask, was filled with alcohol.

In the yard of an ancient church in Maryland rests an old sailor in a hammock. He is buried in an underground tomb beneath a flat stone from which the hammock hangs.

The route by which Colonel Robert Elliott reached the yard of the Presbyterian Church on Twelfth Street in Cincinnati in 1794 was a circuitous one. A marble monument stands there today in his memory. Colonel Elliott was en route west from Hagerstown, Pennsylvania, via Fort Hamilton to Cincinnati. A man of tremendous size, reputed to have weighed three hundred pounds, he was ambushed by Indians on the last leg of his journey and shot to death. Twice after his death, though, he almost got even with the Indians. First, immediately after his murder, warriors attempted to scalp him, and his hair came off in their hands. He wore a wig! After companions had placed his body in a box to take to Cincinnati for burial, his manservant, riding Elliott's horse, was again ambushed, and he was killed. This time the Indians expected to loot the wagon, and they broke open what they thought was a chest filled with valuables—only to find the bald corpse of the Colonel. They unhitched the horses that had pulled the wagon serving as the Colonel's bier, and fled with them.

A gentleman of German extraction had spent most of his life in New York City, where he was fond of fishing on shoals in New York Harbor. His will directed that his remains should be cremated and scattered over his favorite fishing spots. Fellow members of his fishing club claimed large catches afterward.

The captain of the steamship *Elbe* helped to satisfy the last wishes of a man who died in Pittsburgh, Pennsylvania, in 1887, and who had asked to be cremated. The deceased had directed that his ashes be forwarded to the office of the German Consul in New York City, who was to deliver them to the *Elbe* captain.

All of this was done. Then, in midocean, according to instructions, the captain requested all passengers to dress in nautical costume and to stand at attention while he ascended the mast and threw the ashes to the winds.

More than one person has kept the living in mind and provided for their pleasure at the time of a funeral or its anniversary. Carl Schuman, a peddler, had been living at a home for the aged in Cincinnati when he died in 1910. He asked for cremation and suggested that his ashes be tossed to the winds. He also left monies to a social group he had enjoyed, the Herwegh Maennerchor Society, for everyone "to have a good time" after the cremation. His remains, which had been deposited in a golden urn, were scattered in the air, and then the celebration began.

Jerry Hilborn of West Minot, Maine, had the same idea, but he went farther than Schuman. Convivial Jerry left funds for *annual* parties on the anniversary of his death. They were held in his memory for years after he had "slipped his moorings."

A favorite story is told about an eighteenth-century Englishwoman who escaped the grave for years after her death, contrary to her expectations. Martin Van Butchell was a medical practitioner and dentist of questionable ability. When his wife died, he employed the services of Dr. Hunter, celebrated because, as early as the 1700's, he was practicing embalming in England. The corpse was carefully dressed in a linen gown and placed in a special coffin with a glass top, which had been set up in the drawing room of the family residence. Guests who had not known Mrs. Van Butchell in life were introduced by the bereaved husband to his "dear departed." Visiting hours were advertised to the public: "Any day between Nine and One, Sundays excepted." There was, of course, a reason behind all this: The marriage settlement of the "preserved lady" had stipulated that her husband was to have control of her monies "as long as she remained above ground."

Finally Van Butchell remarried, and his second wife objected to sharing him with the first. The "dear departed" was sent to

St. Michael's Cemetery, Charleston, S.C. Wooden marker, center, marks "grave of child about 1775."

the Royal College of Surgeons, where she remained 150 years. In May of 1941 bombs hit the College and left it in ruins.

The recent death, cremation, and distribution of the ashes of Franklin R. Little, publisher of the *Advance News* of Ogdensburg, New York, bring up-to-date burial requests that seem rather untraditional. Mr. Little died on April 20, 1975, and his newspaper published these instructions for his attorney:

> As I told you the Sunday you were up at the hospital, I would like to have my remains cremated, one half buried with Janet in the Ogdensburg cemetery and the other sent to Colorado. I want half of my ashes scattered from an airplane over the Sangre de Christo Range in the West Mountain Valley of Colorado just at sunset when the setting sun has turned that maginficent blood-red which the Spanish explorers described as "Sangre de Christo" or "Blood of Christ." The section where I would like to have my ashes scattered is at the peaks back of the Canda Ranch, where I spent several very happy summers when I was a boy.

It is obvious from some of the unusual directions for funerals and burials that people often give these events considerable

Early cemetery, New Castle, Del.

deliberation. In earlier days, though, before the time when embalming became common, many died and were buried far from home in places they couldn't possibly have anticipated. In many of the cemeteries of Savannah, Georgia, and Charleston, South Carolina, I noticed inscriptions bearing a different place of birth: "born in Philadelphia"; "born in New London, Connecticut"; "born in Ireland"; "an Englishman of London, England."

In *Reminiscences and Sketches*, published in 1890, William Hall wrote about a particularly appealing ancient church and its churchyard burying place:

> If the spirits of the dead take any interest in the last resting place of their mortal remains they must be well content with this. Dry Ridge, Buffalo and Wills Mountains for background. . . . Talk about Westminster Abbey and the crypts of great European cathedrals! Better far this beautiful country home of the dead with its widespread landscape dressed in living green in summer, or wrapped in the pure white sheet of winter snow.
>
> The old church is no longer used as a place of worship except on funeral occasions. . . .
>
> It is a queer old church, standing right in the midst of the encircling graves, with a wine-glass shaped pulpit, just large enough to hold the preacher, who is shut in by a little door on which there is a

wooden turn-bolt, as if there was danger of his escaping—a sort of cage. It is perched on a post and access is had to it by eight or nine steps, and the pews have high straight backs. . . . And there is the funniest little gallery supported by posts, with a floor at an angle of forty-five degrees and three tiers of high-backed pews, and a steep, narrow staircase to get to it. . . .

They have a stove so as to have a fire on cold or rainy days, and a Bible and hymn books, and it is soothing to bury the dead with services in the ancient church in which the forefathers of the hamlet worshiped. Old men and women are laid away in their narrow homes, who, as boys and girls, worshiped and went to Sunday school in the old church, and played among the graves. . . .

The first graves were scattered promiscuously, with no arrangement for walks or family plots. But some years ago the cemetery was incorporated. . . . A large part of it has been laid out in lots where families are buried together, and walks are neatly kept in order by a sexton. They have fourteen acres of ground, and a comfortable dwelling house occupied by the sexton. There have been fifty-eight interments within the last two years. Ah me! how fast the place is filling up! it is far more populous than the adjoining village. As I walked there a short time since in the bright sunshine of an October Sunday, I saw the names of many an old friend. . . . How memories crowded on me as I recalled the past, and saw them all, as they were a few years since, in active business and political life. In the presence of eternity how unsubstantial and unimportant are the things of time.

7

There is rest in Heaven.

GRAVESTONES
AND EPITAPHS

There is a link death can not sever,
Love and memories last forever.

—Old epitaph

When they were first used years ago, grave markers were
shrines to the ghosts of the deceased and were intended to placate
evil spirits. In America gravestones were meant chiefly to identify
grave sites, and they have been used almost since the first interments in colonial days, although few markers from the 1600's
still exist. The most common reason for erecting a marker is obvious; yet such markers have served many purposes. Since they
bear birth and death dates, they have been avidly studied by the
genealogists. In Victorian days tombstones seemed to the ostenta-
tious one last chance to "keep up with the Joneses." The individual stonecutter could even advertise his skill in a masterpiece
of mortuary carving. In the Springdale Cemetery in Ohio, a
stone states: "Here lies Jane Smith, wife of Thomas Smith,
Marble cutter, Monuments of the same style, $350."

Poured cement markers in the Shingle Creek Cemetery near Kissim-mee, Fla.

Worn stones replaced by new ones in St. Michael's Cemetery, Charleston, S.C. The new stone is fastened to the old.

Crude early marker is merely a boulder telling us "Ma dyed." Old
Deerfield Cemetery, Deerfield, Mass.

Today American gravestones are gaining new respect as art
forms, so that stones and rubbings of stones have been exhibited
at museums and art galleries. Some have been accepted as among
the most imaginative of our folk-art sculptures. Gravestone
"rubbing" is becoming a popular hobby; everyday folks, not just
art critics, are interested in these readily accessible art objects.

Our ancestors, through expediency, used many means to mark
the graves of their loved ones: a board; a heap of stones or a
single boulder; a slab of slate, schist, marble, limestone, green-
stone, granite, mica stone, or red or brown sandstone. In early
colonial days and especially in the country, there were no commercial stones, and a family made its own crude markers. A
marker made of glass is cautiously preserved in the Old Fort
Museum at Schoharie, New York. A small red boulder in Old
Deerfield Cemetery, Deerfield, Massachusetts, says simply, "Ma
Dyed Novem 7 Anno 1696."

There are handmade, homemade twentieth-century burial
markers, too. Most are made from poured cement, like those in
Shingle Creek Methodist Cemetery near Kissimmee, Florida.
These exist in whatever shape took the maker's fancy. One has
a place for a photograph and stands for flower pots at each
side. There is a heart made from marbles stuck in wet cement.
On the ones I have seen the lettering is crude, the spelling primi-

tive. Some inscriptions are: "Lan at rest," "Gone but not for-gotten," "Standen at the cross."

Old-time stonecutters had a tedious job. After cutting out a likely piece of stone with drill and sledge, they had to haul it, probably by horse and stone boat, to the workshop. The method of making this chunk of stone into a small slab or slabs de-pended in part on the type of stone. One method used in early days was to lay a line of vinegar and douse this with cold water, splitting the rock. A gravestone could then be roughly hewn with a toothless saw. When a crude representation of the desired

Early sandstone markers are frequently worn by weather. This stone, in good condition, is in Old Deerfield Cemetery.

Old stone in Colonial Cemetery, Savannah, Ga., shows stonecutter's marks on back of stone which have not been smoothed down.

The winged head was a popular symbol in the eighteenth century, and slate was a material used for many early markers. This one is in Old Deerfield Cemetery.

These wooden markers, weathered too much to show an inscription, are stark and lovely. Boggy Creek Cemetery, near St. Cloud, Fla.

shape had been achieved, the stonecutter got out his chisels and mallets and laboriously chipped away the material he didn't want. A marker could be smoothed by polishing it with sand and water and another stone.

Slate is softer and was easier to work. Because it forms in layers, the stonecutter could split it to the desired thickness. He then scratch-carved the designs and letters with mallet and chisel, or sometimes he sculptured the slate, leaving a bas-relief portrait, a border of acanthus leaves, and a rim for a frame.

A wood carver, Stan Ion Petras, recommended using wood for cemetery markers, suggesting, "Wood, eventually beaten and weathered by the sun, wind, rain, is a better symbol, a gradual return to the elements. It shows humans encountering death like

The wooden marker for a child's grave. Boggy Creek Cemetery, near St. Cloud, Fla.

the tree encounters winter." I have seen wooden markers that were elegant in their simplicity and others, more complex, that resembled the head of a bed. The inscriptions on such markers, though, are quickly erased by time.

Markers over the years have appeared in several forms. There are simple headstones with their accompanying smaller footstones. There are also large family monuments. In earlier days "wolf stones" were used: these were large flat stones that covered more than one grave and were intended to discourage marauding

Marble was also used at an early date. This is in Bennington Center Cemetery, Bennington, Vt.

Table tombs. Old Deerfield Cemetery, Deerfield, Mass.

Family tomb of James Hunter, dated 1839, Colonial Cemetery, Savannah, Ga. Coffins were usually stacked in such tombs.

This double marker is in the French style. Circular Congregational Cemetery, Charleston, S.C.

Cement enclosure around single grave. Shingle Creek Methodist Cemetery, near St. Cloud, Fla.

animals. The Moravians in our country used breast stones, all the same size, laid flush with the ground. Table stones, which stood free on four legs, with inscriptions on the top like those in the cemetery of Old Deerfield, were frequently used in early times. Then there have been all kinds of sarcophagi, plain and fancy, that look like vaults above ground but usually aren't. These appear, for instance, in the yard of Immanuel Episcopal Church in New Castle, Delaware.

Every cemetery seems to have its own family vault, a walk-in tomb, above or below ground. Smaller, single brick tombs can also be found; one, in Saint Michael's Cemetery in Charleston, shows a sheet-iron half cylinder above ground. In the mid-nineteenth century grave markers "in the French style" were popular. They were constructed like a bed with head and foot pieces and side rails; inside the structure flowers were planted.

Family plots within cemeteries have been enclosed by every method imaginable: stone walls, brick walls, hedges, picket fences, and solid concrete walls. The iron fences show the most variety, their innumerable designs ranging from the conventional ones to specially designed urns and harps. In Perth, New York, first

Iron fencing used in Colonial Cemetery, Savannah, Ga.

settled by immigrants from Perthshire, Scotland, there is an enclosure of iron fencing in the pattern of Scottish thistles. The simplest boundary marker I have seen was a single strand of chain stretched between wooden posts.

Charles Baldwin of Catskill, New York, was a stonecutter during the last half of the nineteenth century. He left journals, which are now in the New York State Library. Unfortunately

Charles Baldwin mentioned cutting a wreath "in hard Italian marble." Cemetery in Edinburg, N.Y.

for the person interested primarily in his occupation, Baldwin filled his notebooks with reports of young ladies he was fond of, and devoted less space than one might hope to stonecutting. A few notes, however, are helpful:

June 5, 1867. Saugerties: Worked at Nelson Brainerd's Marble Shop carving a wreath of flowers for him. [During the evening Baldwin and Brainerd visited the local cemetery.]

July 30: This afternoon I completed the wreath I have been carving, and am now engaged in carving a bunch of Scotch Thistles. Rather an odd job.

Aug. 1: Finished Scotch Thistles and also cut a line of Rustic Letters . . . then I gathered up my tools and walked to the ferry.

Sept. 10: I have worked today on a wreath of flowers on a very hard piece of Italian marble.

Sept. 14: This forenoon I finished the panel of Rustic Letters (George W. Fraleigh) and finished out the day at ordinary work.

Sept. 20: Today I cut a panel of Rustic Letters (Henry Laurence Family) on a monument die. Then commenced cutting a small wreath. Worked on a monument cap.

[At about this time Baldwin entered a carved medallion, which he called "Memory," in a fair at Hudson. He complained that the medallion was "heavy lugging" as he carried it to the boat *City of Hudson* en route to and from the fair.]

Nov. 8: Father, George Bender and I came to Albany this forenoon. . . . It was quite a spell before we could obtain Trucks to carry the monument and did not get them loaded until noon. We took dinner at the steamboat and at half past one o'clock started for the Cemetery about two-and-a-half miles from the city. At the Cemetery we had some trouble finding the Holcomb lot and it was three o'clock before we started putting it up. The Derrick we used was not a suitable one and that hindered us greatly. We worked until night to get the Plynth and Base in position. Then we went about three-fourth of a mile to the nearest Hotel.

Nov. 9: . . . returned to Albany Rural Cemetery and went to work. We got through soon after noon, and then took passage in a horse-cart to Albany.

May 20, 1868. Fair Haven, Vermont: Sold two carved medallions to Adams and Allen for $250, each, and rec'd order for a second pair.

[Charles and his father also picked out a new supply of marble here.]

Apr. 5: George Bender and his two sons were setting a monument in the Cemetery today. The monument was upset by a crowbar and fell on the youngest boy. (The stone weighed 1200 pounds.) The upper end hit a mound of ice fortunately. The boy has a severe cut on the back of his head and the bridge of his nose is broken.

Apr. 19, 1869: I passed a pleasant season with Sarah Alger at her home in Hudson. . . . I gave her a beautiful marble box I had made for her.

In Scotch Plains, New Jersey, a stonecutter marked the stones he cut with his name, "Osborn," a tiny signature hidden in a corner. Quite a few cutters signed their work—often at the bottom on the right. Unfortunately stones sink, and many signatures have probably been lost beneath the ground. Some stonecutters initialed their work, at times quite prominently.

As folks gain more interest in gravestones, as art objects or to "rub," more sculptors are being discovered. William Parkham, Henry and John Stevens, Henry Christian Geyer, John Gand, and William Mumford worked around Boston; the Foster family worked in Dorchester, Massachusetts; the Lamson family

Sculptor's name shows at bottom of stone in cemetery near Galway, N.Y.—"P. Hood, Sch'dy."

This marker is in a cemetery near Galway, N.Y.

in Charlestown. In Deerfield, Massachusetts, Solomon Asley plied his trade; in Harvard, Massachusetts, the Worcester family. Also in Massachusetts, William Young was in Tatunck, Matthew Girswold in Lynn, Marin Woods in Whately, and Beza Soule and his family in Brookfield. In Cumberland, Maryland, there was A. Amick; in Pennsylvania, Abram and Christian Funk. J. S. Haines worked in Keyser, West Virginia, and a man named McKindrick in Winchester, Virginia. In the churchyards of Charleston, South Carolina, grave markers are signed by J. White, E. R. White, and W. T. White, J. Hall, T. Walker, C. Melville, and G. Runne. Matthew Hood made stones in Albany, New York, and P. Hood marked his "P. Hood, Schdy" (for Schenectady).

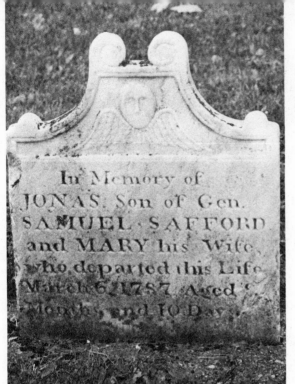

The shape and sculpture on this comparatively simple stone is particularly effective. Bennington Center Cemetery, Bennington, Vt.

Samuel Pennypacker, once governor of Pennsylvania, told a story that reminds us of one of the problems of the stonecutter. Pennypacker quoted a farmer acquaintance who was discussing his neighbor's long name: "Dat name, Truckenmiller, iss so long dat ve chust calls them T-Miller, and ven dey gets buried up in Keeley's crave-yard, dat iss vat goes on the cravestones!"

The lettering on today's marble and granite stones is precise and carefully executed, but not nearly as appealing as the quaint, difficult-to-read lettering on early stones. Inexplicable abbreviations, unexpected capitals, words run together, and *s*'s that look like *f*'s add to the charm. Half-size letters are inserted as hints —M^{rs}, NOV^r, Jan^y—so that we can usually guess what the carver intended. Corrections or additions or downright errors are much in evidence. Stones were reused, just chiseled down so that inscriptions could be cut deeper, and in this case, the first chisel marks can sometimes be seen. At times chiseling down was done for an individual letter when the cutter made a mistake. A

This quadruple stone marks the burial place of the children of Levy and Esther Hathaway in the Bennington Center Cemetery.

gravestone in Norfolk, Virginia, which starts "Sacred to the Memory of Mrs. Margaret . . ." has a note at the bottom: "Erratum, for Margaret read Martha."

Words were misspelled or spelled in the contemporary British fashion, especially on really early stones: "flour" for "flower," "boddy" for "body," "mournfull" with two l's, and "dye" and "lye" with *y*'s rather than *i*'s. Letters or words were omitted and inserted with a caret. In Schoharie County, New York, a bereaved husband instructed the stone carver to cut "Forever Thine" on his wife's headstone. The carver was careless in figuring his space; the marker reads "Forever Thin." Misplaced marks of

This is a double marker for Joanna and William Arms, who died in 1729 and 1731, respectively. Old Deerfield Cemetery.

"And when the last trumpet sounds,
Arise, come forth, ye Dead . . ."
Old Deerfield Cemetery.

Skeleton symbol on the headstone of Thomas Poole, castaway on the bar of Charleston Harbor in 1754. Epitaph says: "Yesterday for me Today for Thee." Circular Congregational Church, Charleston, S.C.

punctuation add to our confusion or our amusement. The formality of the wording, too, is sometimes a shock: "In memory of Mrs. Sarah Wheeler, wife of Mr. Elisha Wheeler," "To the memory of Mr. Jared Abenethy is this stone erected." Sometimes there is lettering on two sides of a marker, perhaps the name on one, the epitaph on the other. Marion Rawson, in *Candleday Art,* asks, "Are we to believe that the old stonecutters knew what they were about artistically, when they left irregular spaces, chipped a mark through a wrong date, crowded lines up to the very edge of a stone, and yet left masterpieces?"

When we consider the lettering on the stones in a single burying ground, we might be looking at a printer's style sheet. There is infinite variety—from beautiful script reminiscent of calligraphy, to Gothic lettering, Roman lettering, German and Old English styles.

There have been periods in gravestone ornamentation—beginning with the horrid skulls and crossbones, skeletons, and hour glasses that have run out of time in the Pilgrim century, changing to winged cherubs, angels, and attempts at realistic

Clock, crossbones, pick and shovel decorate the top of this marker
in Old Deerfield Cemetery.

Skull and crossbones mark this segment of stone preserved in the
Colonial Cemetery in Savannah, Ga.

Slate portrait stone, Circular Congregational Cemetery, Charleston, S.C.

Angel blows trumpet on Margaret Elford stone. St. Philip's Episcopal Cemetery, Charleston, S.C.

Enlargement of motif on Elford stone.

portraiture in the eighteenth century. Harold Eberlein and Abbot McClure in *The Practical Book of Early American Arts and Crafts* comment on the work of the stonecutter of the latter period:

> . . . but he managed to inject not a little variety into his interpretations of these lugubrious emblems of mortality. There were dolorous cherubs and merry cherubs and fat, mumpy-cheeked celestial youngsters joyously fluttering their robust little wings; cherubs with their ambrosial locks done up in puffs that would have put the most proficient Parisian *friseur* to unending and envious shame. Occasionally the cherubs were dour of visage, and there is one creature, done in scratch or incised carving, on a mica-stone in St. Thomas' churchyard, Whitemarsh, Pennsylvania, with a frilled head dress and three-cornered ears, whose aspect is positively devilish. No wonder Lord Howe's soldiers, when they were encamped on St. Thomas's Hill, used this vixenish object as a target for pistol practice. The majority of cherubs, however, were apt to be phlegmatic and stupid looking.

Next, in the nineteenth century, came wreaths, swags, urns, weeping willows, birches, and elms, with a scattering of doves

Portrait stones seem to indicate an attempt at realistic representation of the deceased. These stones are usually eighteenth century and made of slate. Circular Congregational Cemetery, Charleston.

The simple geometric design is found in more than one area. This is from Old Deerfield.

and lambs and hands with pointing fingers. One stone with a finger pointing down suggests simply, "When I die, bury me here." There are symbolic triangles representing faith, hope, and charity, and all-seeing eyes. There are hearts, crosses, crowns, limbs broken from their trunks, and flower stems severed in the middle.

Even the early stones with their ugly ornaments sometimes had borders more beautiful in thought and form than the main decorations. There were motifs that suggested the glories of afterlife—a rope to signify eternity, a rising sun to indicate resurrection, fruits for abundance, laurel leaves, emblems of victory.

An excerpt from a letter comments: "We have just got his gravestone home but I think we can not set it till the ground is settled. It cost $16, the rose and bud, a broken branch, an eight-line verse." This stone was for a seven-year-old who had died, his doctor-father thought, from "flux and fever."

A bridal wreath broken by a dart showed that the deceased was a young bride or groom; a sheaf of wheat or a shattered urn was used for the aged. Willows expressed sorrow; an upright cypress, hope; the evergreen leaves of a yew, eternal life. Doorways and gateways on stones reminded viewers that death is the open door to afterlife. Grapes and their vines represented Christ. The scallop shell was a symbol of man's journey through life. The emblems of fraternal organizations indicated the membership of the deceased.

During the late 1800's stones became large, ornate, pretentious. Twentieth-century markers, especially in the South, sometimes have photographs of the dead on them.

The symbol found on the grave marker of Captain Elias Rich is fascinating because it was not man-made. Elias was a pious man who tried his utmost to live by the Good Book, and he was proud of his endeavors. Probably he was disagreeably self-righteous as far as his family and neighbors were concerned. Whenever he had anything to say, he ended his conversation with "You know, when I die, I'm going to have a heavenly crown,"

Markers in the second half of the nineteenth century became ornate and as gingerbready as Victorian architecture. Bonaventure Cemetery, Savannah, Ga.

Twentieth-century markers, especially in Southern states, sometimes carry photographs of the deceased. Boggy Creek Cemetery, near St. Cloud, Fla.

Crowned heads are sometimes found on gravestones. Perhaps the crown is one of righteousness. Old Deerfield Cemetery.

The symbol of the open coffin is unusual. This marker says: ". . . on her left Arm lieth her Infant Wich was Still Born." Old Deerfield Cemetery.

This is in memory of two Swift children who died in 1700. Bennington Center Cemetery.

and he became, to all of his associates, "Heavenly Crown" Rich. All of this is described in a poem by Horban Day included in *Pine Tree Ballads*, part of which follows:

> Elias Rich would kneel at night
> By the wooden kitchen chair,
> He would clutch the arms and bow his head,
> And pray his evening prayer.
> And the prayer was ever the same old plea
> Repeated for two-score years,
> "Oh Lord, most high, please hear my cry
> From this vale of sin and tears.
> I hain't no-count and I hain't done much
> That's worthy in thy sight.
> But I've done the best I could, Dear Lord,
> According to my light.
> I did as much for my fellowman
> As really, Dear Lord, I could,
> Considerin' my pay is a dollar a day,

And I've earned it choppin' wood.
I've never hankered no greed on earth
For more'n my food and roof,
And all the meat I've had to eat
Was cut near horn and hoof.
But I figure, Dear Lord,
That I've earned my way
And never been on the town,
And when I die and go up high,
I'll wear my heavenly crown.

Old Elias' wife hadn't heard "the call," and she wasn't nearly as positive as Elias that he'd wear his coveted crown. Certainly there were things more important, she thought, than his continual prayers.

Old "Heavenly Crown" died. After his headstone had been set, folks visiting the cemetery were astounded to notice a change in the face of the stone. In an area left unmarked by the

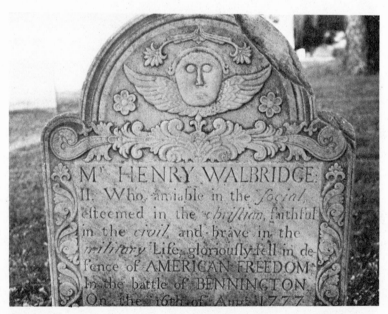

Bas-relief sculpture is profuse on the marker of a soldier killed during the Revolutionary War. Bennington Center Cemetery.

Unusual head with an Egyptian look ornaments this marble marker in the North Cemetery, Galway, N.Y.

stonecutter's chisel, the outline of a head resembling Elias appeared, wearing—of course!—that heavenly crown. The subtle portrait was so true to life it could be recognized. According to legend, this was just too much for Widow Rich, who scrubbed the stone at night with sand and brush—only to see by the next sun that the head with its crown remained to mock her. Old Elias had won!

When churches were first built in America, and churchyards started filling with their founders, it was not the material or the shape of the marker that was important, but the epitaph. These words of warning, with important graphic symbols (for many people could not read), were meant to be studied and taken seriously.

171

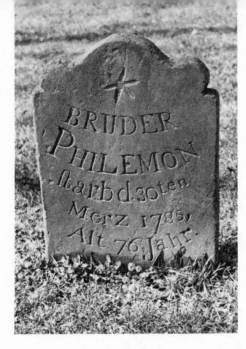

This marker is from the Ephrata Cloister Cemetery, Ephrata, Pa.

All ye who read with little care,
Who walk away and leave me here,
Should not forget that you must die
And be entombed, as well as I.

By me Mortality is taught,
Your days will pass like mine.
Eternity, Amazing Thought,
Hangs on this Thread of Time.

Behold the glass, Improve thy time
For mine is Run and so must thine.
I have found Godliness Great Gain,
So Run till you the Prize Obtain.

Learn this, ye gay,
That life's a transcient flower,
Which grows, and fades,
And withers in an hour.

Death's cold imbraces you must try,
And leave the world, as well as I.

How lov'd, how valu'd once, avails me not,
To whom related, by whom begot.
A heap of dust alone remains of me,
'Tis all I am, and all the proud shall be.

GRAVESTONES AND EPITAPHS

Here lies the form of Uncle Ruf,
Who lived and died searching for truth,
Here let me rest and here repose,
While green grass o'er my body grows.
Let no rude hands remove the stones,
And cursed be him who sees my bones.

In memory of the Reverend M. Jedediah Dewey
First pastor of the Church in Bennington who after
a Laborious Life in the Gospel Ministry Resigned his
Office in God's Temple for the Sublime Employment
of Immortality December 21, 1778 in the 65th year
of his Age.

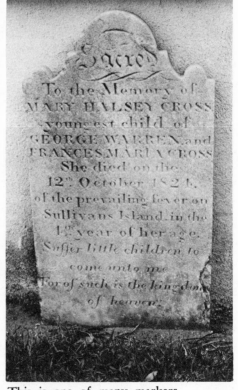

This stone is a eulogy to the
Reverend Tennant. St. Michael's
Cemetery, Charleston, S.C.

This is one of many markers
that explain the cause of death.
St. Michael's Cemetery, Charleston, S.C.

Of comfort no man speaks
Let's talk of graves and worms
and epitaphs. Make dust our paper
and with rainy eyes write Sorrow
in the Bosom of the Earth.

> Here lies buried
> Mrs. Eunice Felton
> Who quitted Mortality
> May 25, 1786
> In the 38th year of her age.

Tender love is the theme of numerous sayings and verses used as epitaphs:

> May God be kind to Elizabeth,
> For she was kind to God.

> Sleep, Lovely Babe, and take thy rest.
> God called thee early because he liked thee best.

> Warm southern sun,
>   shine softly here,
> Warm southern wind,
>   blow lightly here.
> Green sod about, lie light,
>   lie light,
> Goodnight, dear Father,
>   Goodnight, Goodnight.

Some epitaphs are biographies. This is from the marker of Captain James Elford in the cemetery of the French Protestant Church in Charleston:

> In memory of a native of Bristol, England, But for many years a respectable citizen of the United States who died in Charleston on the 25th of January, 1826, aged 54 years. When this experienced and successful sea captain retired from navigation, it was only to study and reveal its theory and lend the lights of his genius to his Brethren of the Ocean. He was the

Child's monument. Cemetery near Rye, N.H.

Birds often decorate markers for children. Cemetery on Green Corner's Road, off Route 29 to Saratoga, N.Y.

author of several scientific, nautical inventions, particularly of an admirable system of marine telegraph signals which afford the sea the same facilities of language as the land. He was prosperous and happy in domestic life and his widow and twelve children mourn his decease.

Skilled in the stars, in the useful learning wise,
He served the earth by studying the skies.
He knew them well—his blest pursuits were given.
He studied first—and then, he entered, Heaven.

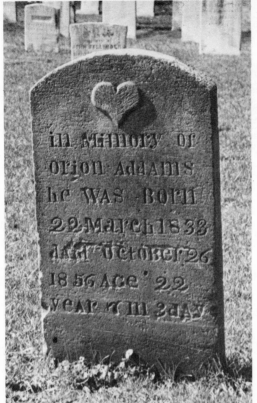

The heart symbol is used in different ways. The simple heart here is effective. Notice the varying type in the inscription. Ephrata Cloisters Cemetery.

This was once a beautiful slate marker. Stoney Creek Cemetery, southwest of Savannah, Ga.

GRAVESTONES AND EPITAPHS

This inscription contains the elements for a novel:

Here lie the remains of the Hon. Robert Daniell, a brave man who had long served King William in his wars, both land and sea, and afterwards governed this province under the lords proprietors. He died on the first day of May in the year 1718, aged 72 years.

Here also was buried the body of Martha Logan who was first the wife of the above Robert Daniell and afterwards of Colonel George Logan of his Majesty's army and also the bodies of his son, George Logan, and his son's wife, Martha, who was the daughter of the Hon. Robert Daniell.

The horse on Susan's marker is rare. Cemetery on Green Corner's Road, off Route 29 to Saratoga, N.Y.

This urn and vine are beautifully cut. They were often used in the 1800's. Colonial Cemetery, Johnstown, N.Y.

DEATH IN EARLY AMERICA

Some epitaphs relate an incident in the life of the dead, or recount the greatest achievements of the deceased:

Sacred to the memory of Hugh McCall
Brevet Major in the United States Army
Born in North Carolina February 17, 1767
Died June 10, 1824.

He served the United States in various capacities 30 years, the last twenty under severe bodily suffering but with usefulness to himself, his Country and his friends.

Major McCall wrote the first history of Georgia. The first volume was published in 1811 and the second in 1816.

Ship ornaments were favored on the grave markers of seafaring men. St. Philip's Episcopal Cemetery, Charleston, S.C.

The rising sun was a popular symbol of the eighteenth and nineteenth centuries. Stoney Creek Cemetery, southwest of Savannah, Ga.

GRAVESTONES AND EPITAPHS

James Scout died Feb. 1829, aged 90 years, 6 months.
He was a brave soldier in Washington's army.
He was an intimate friend of Thomas Paine, who was
in the same army. He shot an Englishman 900 yards
from him and killed him.

Under his command 1400 Confederates defeated 6000
Federals at Honey Hill, Nov. 30, 1864.

In memory of Captain Ben Fitch:
An officer valiant, bold and brave
His life he risked our rights to save.
At Bridgewater Battle a wound he received,
Yet held fast the banner till he was relieved.

Other verses recall marital bliss and love for a mate:

Farewell, bright soul, a short farewell;
Till we shall meet again above
By the sweet groves, where
Pleasure dwells and trees of life
Bear fruits of love.

We had together many years,
Together now we lie,
Together may we rise with joy
To mansions in the sky.

We took sweet counsel together and
walked unto the house of God in company.

Other epitaphs tell the story of more than one marriage:

Here lies a wife
Of two husbands bereft:
Robert on the right,
Richard on the left.

The uprooted tree appeared on numerous nineteenth-century markers. St. John's Lutheran Cemetery, Charleston, S.C.

In memory of Jane and Ama Sweetman
1st and 2nd wives of
Rev. Joseph Sweetman.

Jane died Jan. 27, 1802
Aged 25 years

Ama died Mar. 15, 1827
Aged 56 years

Strangers in life,
Our dust mingles in the grave.

In one graveyard three bodies lie side by side, a husband and his two wives. In the center of the husband's marker, hands point toward each side, with the word "Mine." Each stone beside it has a single hand, finger pointed toward the middle, with the word "Ours."

Sometimes an epitaph explains the cause of death:

> Here lie Paul, Rachel, Amos, John and tiny Richard,
> put to an early death by the misability of sister
> Elizabeth to light a fire in the hearth.

> In memory of Jesse Emory Purle
> Taken from this life by naebody's fault but her own.
> On hearing a child scream, she sprang from her chair,
> Leaving it still agog. May the Lord snatch her
> From the hand of the Devil.

Does the above refer to the superstition that to leave a chair rocking empty is to invite death?

> Jonathan Weaver
> Died while following his plow
> of a Polypus seated on the Aorta.

> The pains of childbirth
> Was her end.
> The cause did
> From Eve descend.

> Joan, daughter of Joseph and Edith Hill
> died at this spot by her husband's tomahawk.
> God rest her sole.

Faith, Hope, and Charity appear on this mid-nineteenth-century stone in an Edinburg, N.Y., cemetery.

In memory of William Harmon
He fell in the service of his country
At the Battle of Wilderness Mountain.

Other causes of death listed on tombstones include "died with ye Small Pox," "killed by a fall from a horse," "died of the prevailing fever," "drowned in the Savannah River," "died of pulmonary affection," "killed by a falling tree," and "died from an organic disease of the chest."

These sentiments show consideration for orphans:

Dear wife for me no sorrow take
But love my child for its father's sake.

Some stones with hands pointing heavenward say merely "Gone home." Shingle Creek Methodist Cemetery, near Kissimmee, Fla.

Thankful Hunt's gravestone is in the cemetery at Edinburg, N.Y.

Picture of Health by Sickness worn
Death takes him from the busy Stage,
And leaves frail Nature here to mourn
The Widow's lot, and Orphans' tender age.

A few epitaphs defy the definition published in Richard
Puttenham's *The Arte of English Poesie*: "An epitaph is an inscription such as a man may commodiously write or engrave
upon a tombe in few verses, pithie, quicke, and sententious, for
the passerby to judge upon without any long tariaunce." The
following cannot be quickly understood:

John H. Marvin died Dec. 30, 1867, Aged 49 years
Ask those who knew him.

Passing stranger call it not,
A place of fear and gloom.
I love to linger o'er the spot,
It is my husband's tomb.

Were the next two epitaphs composed ahead of time by the
deceased?

Here lies the body of Jonathan Fiddle.
On the 30th day of June, 1868
He went out of tune.

Here is where poor Henry lies,
Nobody weeps and nobody cries.
Where he went and how he fares,
Nobody knows and nobody cares.

These are more reassuring:

Harriet Miles
Fell asleep in Jesus
January 16, 1857
Aged 15 years.
Her last word was HAPPY.

Among the most artistic markers anywhere are those in the Ephrata Cloisters Cemetary. Many stones here appear to be of a red standstone.

HIER LIGT BRIDER
FRIED: KELLER,
STARB NOV: 10
1771. ALT 34 IAHR
10 MONAT.

Sacred to the memory of Margaret Charlotte Elford who departed this life May 19, 1817
Aged 45 years 4 months and 20 days leaving a husband with several small children to lament their irreparable loss. She was

In Childhood Obedient
In Wedlock Virtuous
In Prosperity Humble
In Adversity Resigned
In Sickness Patient
In Death Happy.

There are, around the countryside, several grave markers commemorating the burial of a *part* of a body. In Washington Village, New Hampshire, Samuel Jones, a carpenter, was caught between heavy timbers while building the town hall. A marker in the local cemetery finishes the episode: "Here lies the leg of Captain Samuel Jones which was amputated July, 1807." And in Newport, Rhode Island, a stone has been erected to the memory of Wait and William Tripp and to "His Wife's Arm, Amputated February 20th, 1786."

In the 1800's Orvil Teasel ran a tavern between Orwell and Sandbanks in upper New York State. He was known for his sense of humor and jolly manner. One night when business was slow around the tavern, a n'er-do-well appeared at the door asking for a meal and a place to sleep. Teasel invited him inside, offered him a drink on the house, and tried to find out whether he could get some return for his hospitality.

"Ain't there anything you can do to earn a night's lodging, mister?"

The tramp explained that he'd been in the war and had been pretty shot up; since then he hadn't been able to do much work. By that time the few men at the bar felt sympathetic, and they urged Teasel to let the old veteran have bed and board.

Finally the fellow admitted, "About the only thing I can do well is make up poetry."

Teasel thought he saw a chance for some fun and said he'd like the man to compose an epitaph for him. At this prospect the tramp brightened and got busy:

> Here lies a man who died of late,
> And was borne by angels to Heaven's gate . . .

The poet stopped writing, said he was hungry and tired and would really appreciate his supper. He promised to finish the poem in the morning.

Teasel fed him and sent him off to a back room.

There is a small crown at the top of this stone. The flowers at the upper corners are tulips. Ephrata Cloisters Cemetery.

A 1752 slate portrait marker of Mary Dart. Circular Congregational Cemetery, Charleston, S.C.

An enlargement of the Mary Dart marker.

The tramp slept long and well, arose, and ate a leisurely breakfast. Upon the innkeeper's insistence, he got pencil and paper to finish the epitaph, complaining, "The bed was lumpy and your vittles none too good, but I'll stick to my bargain." After a bit he handed his host this verse:

> Here lies a man who died of late
> And was borne by angels to Heaven's gate,
> Then up stepped the Devil, as sly as a weasel,
> And down into Hell he pitched old Teasel.

8

BODY SNATCHING

The body-snatchers! they have come,
   And made a snatch at me;
It's very hard—them kind of men
   Won't let a body be!
Don't go to weep upon my grave,
   And think that there I'll be;
They haven't left an atom there
   Of my anatomy.

Today the thought of stealing bodies from their newly dug graves seems not only grotesque but irrational. Suppose, though, that you had been a doctor eager to learn about human anatomy in the days when there were no textbooks or anatomical charts, when dissection was illegal, and when the general population was so unaware of the knowledge a physician needed that one village voted never to sponsor a doctor who had taken part in dissecting a human body. This happened in New Hampshire in 1820.

The desire of a medical student to study a skeleton was not trivial in the time before classes in anatomical science and skeletons in the closets of high school classrooms became common. The memoirs of the Reverend John Todd, once an apprentice doctor, makes this clear. He says:

> At the age of 22 I found myself, with another stu-
> dent, and with a medical book protruding from each
> pocket, fairly on the track of my profession at old
> Dr. Sale's. . . . I now began to find real difficulties.
> I had very few books, had never seen the skeleton or
> frame of the human body, and had never witnessed a
> surgical operation, or a body being dissected. Oh if I
> could have had a skeleton to look at for a single hour!

At about this time the young student heard an old hunter
mention that he and a companion had found a corpse in the
woods and buried it. Todd queried the man in detail in order to
learn the exact location of the grave, which had been marked
with some cobblestones. Todd was discouraged to hear that the
grave was in the heart of the Adirondacks near Cranberry Lake
and would probably be impossible to locate. After deliberation,
however, he decided to try. His journey, by guide boat with
frequent portages, took him from Lower Saranac Lake to the
Raquette River, where he headed on afoot. There were panthers
and an Indian hunting party in the area. Both frightened Todd,
but after walking all day, he found Cranberry Lake and the
cairn. Returning to Todd's own words:

> How I found the poor stranger's grave and exulted
> as a miser would have done over gold, and how I
> worked and toiled and finally got the bones, every
> one of them! into my bag and on my back, I shall
> not attempt to describe. It cost me three days' hard
> work, and work not the most pleasant.

Starting back out of the woods, Todd lost his way. His sup-
plies ran out, because he had spent twice as long as he had
expected. The cries of wolves were added to those of the
ever-present panthers, and his bullet pouch held only seven balls.
He could not start a fire, either, and during one long agonizing
night, John Todd wondered whether he, too, might become
a corpse to be found by a wandering woodsman and buried in a
shallow grave.

Todd's fervent prayers and the morning light brought hope and energy enough for him to climb a mountain from which he could identify Tupper Lake and figure his route. During the next five days he found his boat, killed a deer for food, and returned safely to Lower Saranac Lake. He had traveled at least 250 miles in a circuitous route and had taken about two weeks to capture his prize. But as John Todd himself says:

> . . . [I] was out of the woods and my treasure with me. I dared not show it even to the old Doctor; but how I gloated over those bones! studied them! strung them! They were the beginning of my professional knowledge and were worth to me a thousand fold more than their cost.

William T. Morton, one of the first doctors to use ether as an anesthetic, was so fascinated by anatomy that he carried a skeleton on his honeymoon, and his bride awakened one morning to find a third party in bed with them. Morton, who had awakened first, was leaning against his pillow, studying piece by piece the specimen from his bag of bones.

Laymen of the 1700's and 1800's were frightened by outrageous rumors describing how cadavers had been violated and by stories of exceptional cases that were actually true. According to one rumor, a joker had tried to get even with a bigoted friend by placing the corpse of a Negro in his companion's bed. And there were whispers afloat in Louisiana of the New Orleans doctor who had figured in several duels and who was said to use the cadavers of charity patients for target practice, "suspending the bodies at the hospital . . . in order to improve his skill as a marksman."

Then there were incidents like the 1830 Castleton raid. The sexton of a Hubbardton, Vermont, church reported that the recently interred body of Mrs. Penfield Churchill, a much-loved member of the community, had apparently been removed. Upon investigation the suspicion was proved to be a fact, and irate friends and relatives suspected students from nearby Castleton

Medical College. They reported their discovery to Sheriff Dike. The lawman led a mob from Hubbardton to Castleton, demanded entrance from the dean of the school, and stormed the dissecting room searching for Mrs. Churchill's body.

However, the students had been warned a little ahead of time. According to legend, they decapitated the body, and an audacious young man carried the head from the premises under his cloak. They hid the torso under the floorboards, where it was finally discovered by the invaders.

This incident received so much publicity that John M. Currier was inspired to compose "The Song of the Hubbardton Raid." Reading the whole lyric, the reader wonders whether Mr. Currier's first purpose was to express distaste for the affair or to advertise Vermont's prize product.

> In the town of green and purple slates,
> Whoever died for miles around,
> This numerous and savage class,
> This class of savage students,
> Was sure to adorn these tables,
> Their flesh would feed the students' fire,
> In this land of slates and quarries,
> Their friends would deck the graves,
> Deck the mounds with fragrant flowers.
> And drop a tear o'er empty coffins,
> Coffins rifled of their contents,
> In this green Mt. Athens,
> In this town of slate and quarries,
> Quarries of green and purple slates,
> Slates that never fade nor tarnish . . .

In Woodstock, also in Vermont, the local medical school was raided. In that town, very near the New Hampshire border, the faculty felt obliged to make a statement: "We will not use or suffer to be used . . . any human body that will be disinterred *hereabouts;* it may appear to be invidious to set limits but we are willing to say the State of Vermont."

In Connecticut, a similar raid on Yale Medical School had taken place in 1824. Townspeople from New Haven and West Haven were enraged after an empty grave was discovered.

When, in 1827, in Lancaster, Pennsylvania, the town's first mayor, John Passmore, died, at age fifty-five, he weighed 408½ pounds. At that time all coffins were custom-made, and no ready-prepared burial box would ever have held that huge hulk, which was finally carried to the cemetery in an oversize open wagon. At the time folks said that for once the church's sexton did not have to monitor a new grave site for fear medical students would claim it as an experimental corpse.

In a history of St. Peter's Church in Philadelphia from 1753 to 1783 this note appears:

> It having been represented that a body has been taken from out of a grave in St. Peter's Churchyard:
>
> Resolved that the Church Wardens issue an advertisement promising a reward of one hundred fifty dollars to be paid upon conviction of the offenders.

Josiah Carter, sexton of the Old Brick Church in Boston, claimed indignantly that he had once tossed an impudent doctor, who tried to buy a corpse from him, into an open grave and started to cover the struggling young man with dirt.

Announcement of Dr. William Shippen's anatomy lectures in Philadelphia in the 1760's caused so much furor that mob violence was feared. On one occasion the doctor left his carriage just before shots were fired into it. The home of Dr. Shippen's father, where the lectures were held, was shunned by townsfolk as a haunt of body snatchers and disembodied spirits. Students in long cloaks, which proved effective disguises, arrived for lectures after dark by a path that wound up through the backyard from an alley. The dissecting room was stoned more than once, despite Shippen's statement that the cadavers being dissected were all those of suicides, executed criminals, or unknowns assigned to Potter's Field.

There were rumors, also, about a long lonely building that stood by a stone bridge over the Cohocksink at North Third Street, Philadelphia, where black smoke curled up from the chimneys. The bold NO ADMITTANCE sign seemed to confirm the suspicion that this was a warehouse for stolen cadavers "where their flesh was boiled and their bones burnt down for the use of the faculty." Actually the building was a factory where hartshorn, a source of ammonia, was made from boiling oil.

Joseph McDowell, a controversial doctor and lecturer at Transylvania Medical College in Lexington, Kentucky, in the first half of the nineteenth century, was the principal actor in what would have made a marvelous farce for the early stage. He was not a brave man—some said he hid under feather ticks during lightning storms—but he was a show-off and, among other questionable activities, delighted in guiding students on grave-snatching expeditions. When a girl died of a little-known disease, he wanted, and obtained, her cadaver for study. As he stood in the laboratory considering dissection, he heard a mob gathering outside the college building. Through a window he saw the guns and long rope the people carried. McDowell claimed afterward that the ghost of his dead mother guided him at this crucial time. He hid the stolen cadaver and lay down on the empty slab himself, pulling the sheet over his body. The raiders broke into the room and searched it cautiously. They lifted the sheet from McDowell's slab. Fear had turned his complexion sallow and waxen. He held his breath.

"Here is a fellow who died with his boots on. I guess he's a fresh one," said a member of the crowd, as he quickly replaced the covering.

The mob straggled out, leaving McDowell safe.

Near Morgantown, Pennsylvania, stands Welsh Mountain, on top of which there was a lonely burying ground for Negro slaves and later free black men. One of the last interments there was that of a man known as Little Round Top, who had been unpopular with both the black and the white folks in the neighborhood because he dared to live with a white woman. Dr. Minn was the general practitioner in Morgantown, and the doctor frequently asked a local handyman, Johnny Proudfoot, to do odd jobs for him. Soon after the funeral of Little Round Top, Dr. Minn asked Johnny to help him carry a "side of leather" up to his garret workshop. The doctor and his cohort were halfway upstairs when Johnny saw Round Top's feet hanging out of the bundle they were lugging. He turned tail and ran, leaving the doctor to tote the cadaver alone.

The next story is identified with at least two localities, Charlton, New York, and Fair Haven, Vermont. As I first heard the story, a Charlton doctor stopped on a cold, gusty autumn evening at a tavern en route to his home and office. He tied his horse to the hitching post and left his companion, muffled in heavy garments, waiting in the buggy. One of the doctor's cronies, familiar with the doctor's habits and activities, walked carefully up as if to speak to the rider. There was cautious movement around the buggy, and soon the doctor, revived by congenial companionship and a warm toddy or two, came out, untied his horse, and gave her a touch of the whip. His hitherto silent guest spoke up, "Mighty cold tonight, isn't it?" The doctor pulled on the reins and jumped from the buggy in amazed terror. Shouts of glee arose at his sudden exit. The doctor's crony, sitting in the seat beside the driver, pulled a muffler from his face. After suspecting why the doctor had needed a strong drink and why his rider had not accompanied him, he had changed places with a corpse, now lying stiff behind the buggy seat.

Another doctor carrying a stolen cadaver also abandoned his wagon in terror. Joseph McDowell, mentioned earlier, and several students were out getting a fresh anatomical specimen during a storm. After the corpse had been loaded into the back of a wagon, the doctor headed toward the medical laboratory building at Transylvania. The doctor heard a loud report—a gunshot or a clap of thunder. Turning quickly toward the sound, he saw the corpse behind him sitting erect with a revolver in its shriveled hand. Fear accelerated McDowell's flight and delighted the students who had maneuvered the body into its threatening position.

In another escapade Transylvania students snatched a corpse and were caught by vigilantes. They were hurried to the courthouse, where their astute lawyer quoted Genesis so convincingly—"For dust thou art and unto dust shalt thou return"—that the boys were allowed to keep their treasure and merely pay a one-dollar fine for the "dust" they had stolen.

This drama had a second act when two professors at the medical college argued over which had the right to dissect this cadaver. The whole rhubarb became notorious when a duel resulted. One doctor was shot in the groin; his opponent stopped the bleeding and probably saved his life. The two became fast friends after that.

In northern New York a widow suspected that her husband's body had been removed from its tomb and sold. When the deceased was buried, he had been adorned by a unique watch of which he was very proud; it was flashy with a long beautiful chain and a diamond fob. A few days after his burial, his widow heard that a local character, who had often admired the costly timepiece, was wearing one exactly like it. She ordered that the body of her husband be dug up. Disinterment took place immediately, and to the astonishment of everyone, the body was undisturbed. Inexplicably, though, the watch, chain, and fob were missing.

Medical societies were formed in the late 1700's and early 1800's. These soon became active in attempting to force legislation that would permit legal dissection for medical study. In 1824 Connecticut passed a law that allowed medical schools to take possession of unclaimed corpses from its prisons, and in 1831 a Massachusetts law made human dissection legal. These pioneer acts served as models for other states, and before long there was no necessity for grave snatching in the name of science.

9

MOURNING CUSTOMS

To weep too much for the dead is to affront the living.
—Old proverb

Deidrick Van Pronk died in Boston and was buried on Copp's Hill. The widow Van Pronk grieved for her lost mate until her friends feared she would become physically ill. She was lonely and restless and found it difficult to sleep at night until she conceived a unique plan. She asked a carver of figureheads for ships to make her a wooden replica of her husband. She kept the effigy, most of the time, in the sturdy four-poster she and Van Pronk had shared, and finally she was able to rest at night.

The widow Van Pronk started to feel more like herself, and occasionally she left her home to go about her business and see a few friends. She visited a new young shoemaker, and romance again entered her life. Before long the two were wed, and he moved into the Van Pronk home. A week or two after this, servants approached the bride to say that they were out of kindling and would not be able to light the morning fires. The former widow thought for just a moment, then said, "Maybe it is vell enough now, to shplit up old Van Pronk vat ish upshtair."

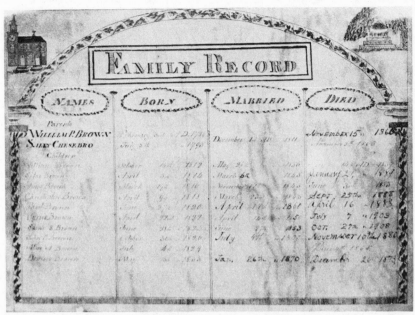

Family record of William Brown and Sally Chesebro.
Courtesy Old Fort Museum, Schoharie, N.Y.

During our earliest colonial days, there was no place for the folderol connected with the later Victorian mourning of the dead. No material was kept on hand to create mourning garb; no book of etiquette suggested where a widow might appear in public and where she might not. Later, after New England churches had been built, funerals were somber affairs accented by an escort of six women, dressed in black, who surrounded the coffin. Sermons were long, and sometimes in the cities they were printed commercially and distributed among friends. As the colonists grew wealthier, they started to use mourning clothes. Men wore flowing black cloaks, generous white scarves, and gloves.

The custom of funeral black is ancient. It originated back in the days when folks felt that spirits, some of them ill-willed, hovered about a corpse. Black was worn to make the living inconspicuous and less apt to be troubled by evil spirits.

Clothing has long been used as an outward symbol of mourning. From Puritan days on, in certain religious communities, such as the Amish and the Mennonites, all of those attending a funeral, not just close relatives, wore black. Men of any sect in earlier times frequently wore dark clothing in or out of mourning, and male mourners were usually identified by the black armbands or hatbands they wore. (A dandy might tie a black ribbon on his cane.) Most of the traditions of mourning garb, however, were prescribed for women.

By the nineteenth century there were definite rules setting the length of mourning and the clothing to be worn during each period. Two years of deep mourning was expected of widows. During the first year the bereaved wore solid black wool gar-

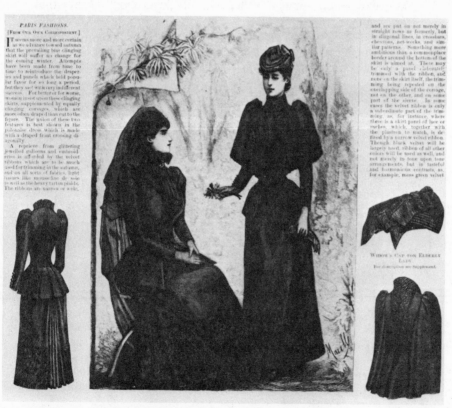

Paris fashion even dictated the styles in mourning dress.

ments—serge, alpaca, or merino—with collars and cuffs of folded, untrimmed crape, no other trim. She might wear a simple crape bonnet—never a hat—and a long, thick, black crape veil. Dark furs were permitted in winter. During the second year of mourning, the widow might wear a silk fabric trimmed with crape and use black lace for her collars and cuffs. She could then shorten her veil and make it of tulle or net. After a year and a half, she might vary her wardrobe with garments or trim of gray, violet, or white. In the last months of mourning, her bonnet might be of lace with white or violet flowers. A widow's hair always had to be arranged simply.

During Victorian times a woman mourning the death of a father or mother or one of her own offspring wore dark clothes for a year. This mourning period lasted half the time a wife traditionally mourned her husband, but the garb was similar.

Memorial locket in velvet case, oil on ivory, circa 1810. In memory of Jacob Lansing, Albany.
Courtesy Albany Institute of History and Art.

Back of the Lansing locket with braided hair of the deceased.
Courtesy Albany Institute of History and Art.

A mourning portrait (1856)
made from a daguerreotype.

Mourning garb was worn for six months for grandparents, for brothers and sisters, and "for a friend who leaves you an inheritance." Mourning for an aunt or uncle or for a nephew or niece was an obligation of only three months, and white trim was allowed throughout.

In deep mourning no kid gloves were permissible, only those made from cotton or silk, or crocheted or knit from thread. During the first months of mourning not even jet beads, traditional trimming in the later stages of mourning, were allowed. The silk fabrics used for dresses, capes, or bonnets had to be lusterless, and any ribbons used were also without gloss. Handkerchiefs used at this time were, when possible, made of only the sheerest white linen, with a broad black border in the deep-mourning period, a narrower band later.

Children in mourning, those under twelve, wore white in summer and gray in winter, both trimmed with black buttons, ruffles, belts, or bonnet ribbons only.

Mourning jewelry was common in the eighteenth and nineteenth centuries, although at the time of the Revolution, when the colonists felt the economic strain of war, jewelry of this

Locket. Miniature on ivory from the Ludlow family, Claverack, N.Y., circa 1830.
Courtesy Albany Institute of History and Art.

type, along with all luxuries, was frowned upon. Jewelry could be worn in memory of the dead long after the traditional mourning period had ended. Men as well as women wore large beautiful gold lockets. These were sometimes ornamented with tiny mourning pictures in black and white of figures weeping over tombs beneath willow trees or birches. Sometimes, though, the locket bore a likeness of the person who had died, a watercolor on paper or on ivory. The inscription, a brief biography, might wind around the frame or be sketched on the back of the case. Andrew Jackson wore such a locket after the death of his beloved Rachel. Each night it rested beside him on a small table, leaning against his Bible.

Locket in memory of Mary Wilkes, born 1764, died 1801.
Courtesy Albany Institute of History and Art.

Back of the Mary Wilkes locket with locks of hair.
Courtesy Albany Institute of History and Art.

A flower spray made of hair, set in a gold frame, was a cherished memento.

Pin or locket. In memory of M. Walsh, August 15, 1792.
Courtesy Albany Institute of History and Art.

There were rings, some of ivory, with typical mourning scenes or symbols. Other jewelry included earrings, pendants, rings, and bracelets in ingenious forms.

There was also jet, used in tiny beads for trim, necklaces in long strings, bracelets, pins, and rings. In some cases jet jewelry was heavy and rather ugly; occasionally it was delicate and lovely.

Activities—of women, especially—during the mourning period were restricted. Women did not attend weddings if in deep mourning and, of course, were not even invited to parties intended to be at all festive.

If a widow or widower felt inclined to remarry, that was usually postponed for a "decent" length of time. The story is told of a deacon in Connecticut whose wife died and was buried. The evening after the funeral, he called on a young lady of the community and asked her to marry him. The young woman, Miss Fellows, was shocked and could not help but show it.

This cartoon illustrates the nineteenth-century preoccupation with mourning customs.

FORMER MISTRESS: "Why, Bridget, for whom are you in black?"
BRIDGET: "For poor Tim, me furrst husband, Mum. When he died I was that poor I couldn't, but I said if iver I could I would, and me new man, Mike, is as ginerous as a lord."

"Why, Deacon, is this not too sudden?"

"Oh, no," explained the deacon, "I picked you out some time ago."

American mourning customs have changed considerably. The depth of our mourning is no longer measured by the blackness of our garb. Today we wouldn't think of dressing a child under twelve in mourning clothes or allowing him to act as a pallbearer. Friends invite the bereaved to concerts or on excursions to divert them, and they accept these invitations. Mourning is no longer a public affair.

10

MEMORIALS

Remember me is all I ask,
And if remembrance be a task,
Forget me.
—From an old autograph album

In Atlanta recently a florist doing business under the name "Flowers for Keeps" was asked to dry a funeral arrangement of mums and roses in the shape of a guitar. This is not as bizarre as many of the memorials that were created to honor friends and relatives in the past. Americans have remembered their dead in a great variety of tangible ways: the wealthy philanthropist by libraries and hospital wings, the common man by one-of-a-kind family records and lockets with miniatures on one side and the precisely braided hair of the deceased on the other. Our ancestors made quilts of black and white to fit their mourning moods and summoned artists without notice to paint their dead or dying loved ones.

A soldier in the Civil War hurried home to have his photograph taken with his dead infant in his arms; he was James Abram Garfield, later our twentieth president. Photographers were frequently called to take pictures of the dead in their coffins.

Large wreaths made of different-colored hair were preserved under glass.

Before the time of cameras and photographs, it was rather common to have a painting made of the deceased or dying if a likeness had not been taken previously. William Gookin, an artist from New Hampshire, advertised in the *Dover Gazette and Strafford Advertiser* during February and March of 1847 that he had hired rooms in Telherly's Block, where he continued his business of portrait, landscape, and fancy painting, and that he would "attend to any calls in the Daguerrean Department with the exception of taking Daguerreotype Miniatures of Deceased Persons," which he insisted "no one can do and give satisfaction to friends of the deceased." He boasted that his method of painting portraits of the deceased and "getting a good Likeness" was well known to the public.

For painting a Dr. Cowan after death, in July 1848, Gookin received forty dollars for the portrait, fifteen dollars for the frame, three dollars "for horse hire," and seven dollars "for time in going." When a child, Hannah Cushing, became ill, her parents

Family record quilt. Members of the family are indicated at top and bottom of covering. As they die, their symbols are moved to the cemetery at the center.

Enlargement of fenced cemetery, complete with shade trees and flowers, at the center of the quilt.

Photo courtesy Kentucky Historical Society, Frankfort.

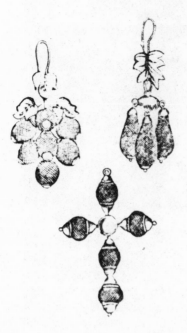

Some examples of jewelry made from the hair of loved ones.

sent a hurried message to Gookin, who went immediately to the Cushing home. Here the mother laid out Hannah's finest dress and called the family pet. Gookin studied the sick child, her garments, and her dog, and returned to his studio to paint the young lady in her best dress against a background of trees with the dog at her feet.

Among the Holland Dutch, especially, it was traditional to inscribe silver spoons, tea sets, trays, and similar creations of the silversmith "In Memory of. . . ." A wealthy grandmother requested in her will that the family jeweler provide matching pieces of silver inscribed in her memory for several of her descendants. At the Albany Institute of History and Art, there is a set of andirons topped by inscribed silver urns, another memorial.

Coffin plates bearing the name of the deceased were sometimes detached and kept as mementos.

Printed handkerchiefs and lithographed pictures, sometimes transferred to Staffordshire china, memorialized the famous dead.

Nathaniel Currier lithograph in memory of Cornelia Vandenburgh,
Half Moon, N.Y., 1846.

Courtesy Albany Institute of History and Art.

Enlargement from a Currier
lithograph in memory of
John Cornell, 1838.
*Courtesy Old Fort Museum,
Schoharie, N.Y.*

An elaborate memorial to George Washington.

It was popular to write elegies for deceased friends. Sometimes the local preacher considered it his responsibility to labor over such a tribute. The verses were attached to the bier or to the hearse, handed out as souvenirs to the mourners, read at the funeral, or published in local newspapers. Charles Baldwin mentioned in his mid-nineteenth-century journals that the minister's poem for Emma, Baldwin's first love, appeared in the Catskill *Examiner*. The elegies were sometimes printed as broadsides, grandly illustrated with such lugubrious symbols as the death's head, skeletons, scythes, all-seeing eyes, and coffins. They were, of course, black-bordered.

Memorials littered Victorian parlors. They sat upon gingerbread stands and upon marble mantels. They hung in shadow boxes. There was a variety of flower memorials, including some made from wax blooms and foliage covered by tall glass cases. Calla lilies were favored. (Proper Victorian funeral flowers were always white or shades of purple, perfect for this romantic age.) Frequently flowers from funeral bouquets were dried, and these, too, were kept under glass. White wax crosses, harps, anchors, and silhouetted heads were shaped and mounted to be used in the same way.

Wreaths of yarn and of seeds were made. Sheaves of wheat tied with flowing ribbons lay upon the coffin until interment and were eventually framed.

Friends presented the bereaved with embossed mourning cards somewhat like today's sympathy cards but more stereotyped and inscribed "In memory of. . . ." These were produced by the makers of lacy valentines.

Memorial wreath made of seeds and artificial berries.
Courtesy Old Fort Museum

Feather wreath memorial.
Courtesy Old Fort Museum

Seeds, nuts, and artificial leaves make this memorial wreath.
Courtesy Old Fort Museum

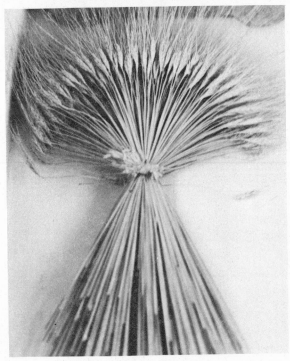

Sheaf of wheat used to ornament a casket before interment, then saved as a memento.
Courtesy Old Fort Museum

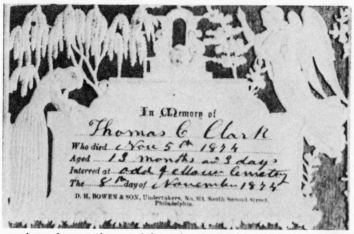

An embossed mourning card featuring popular mourning symbols.

The hair of the dead was woven or braided over fine wire to form imaginative designs and displayed in shadow boxes.

The memorials I find most fascinating, though, are those designed to hang on the parlor or the chamber wall. Such hand-made mourning pictures were popular for about half a century, starting in the late 1700's, although by 1835 lithographers such as Nathaniel Currier were publishing commercial versions of them. Some of the pictures were done by the very young. Most were the work of girls or women, and many were produced in school as assignments in the regular curriculum. Occasionally a memorial painted by a boy is discovered. I suspect that such paintings were suggested by a frantic teacher or mother, perhaps inspired by an engraving already hanging on the wall. The young ladies of the time labored faithfully over these memorials, some for relatives long deceased, some in memory of national heroes. Some of them were made ahead of time for the painter herself or for whatever relative or acquaintance was first to "depart for heavenly spheres." Occasionally uncompleted pictures are found with no inscriptions on the waiting tombs. Had they been used, a mourning card might have been pasted on. Some mourning pictures were needlework exercises with a variety of stitches to

Lock of hair, probably a memorial.
Courtesy Old Fort Museum, Schoharie, N.Y.

give texture and to prove the skill of the embroiderer much as her sampler did.

Symbols for painted or embroidered mourning pictures appeared frequently in copybooks, contemporary magazines, en-

Hair of different colors is wound around fine wire to make intricate blossoms and a bird at the top.
Courtesy Robert Joki Antiques, Saratoga Springs, N.Y.

Weeping willows were often used in mourning pictures to depict sorrow.

Mourning picture of John Jacob Beeckman family. Wool embroidery on silk. New York State, circa 1795.

Courtesy Albany Institute of History and Art.

Mourning picture. Silk embroidery with watercolor on silk. In memory of Mrs. Catherine Matson, New York State, 1807.
Courtesy Albany Institute of History and Art.

gravings, and lithographs, and were used as models. Certain grim symbols were used over and over: tombs, black-garbed mourning figures, weeping trees. Other singular touches were added: pets, ships, a distant town, birds and angels overhead, or churches.

A few memorials made of cut paper have survived. The contrast of black and white is stark and effective. This art, used with superb skill by the Pennsylvania Germans, was apparently not widely used for memorials. The same is true of oils as a medium. A few have been found, not many. Pen-and-ink mourning sketches sometimes appear, and pinpricking can be found, especially in combination with other techniques.

Other mourning pictures were stenciled on velvet. These have mellowed, the velvet itself darkening with age until, in some cases, the whole effect is monochromatic.

Mourning picture. Oil on canvas. Sacred to the memory of Peter and Judith Van Vechten, who died in 1795 and 1791, respectively. New York State.

Courtesy Albany Institute of History and Art.

Mourning picture. Drawing on cotton and wool embroidery. In memory of Gertrude Van Vranken, who died in 1792. New York State.

Courtesy Albany Institute of History and Art.

Mourning picture. Wool and silk embroidery on silk. In memory of
Peter Gansevoort, infant. Albany, 1788.

Courtesy Albany Institute of History and Art.

Mourning picture. Silk and wool embroidery on silk. "Sacred to the
Memory of Rachel Schuyler." This was embroidered by Rachel's
daughter, Angelica. Albany, 1808.

Courtesy Albany Institute of History and Art.

York Springs Churchyard. Oil on canvas, circa 1850. Artist is R. Fibich.

Photo courtesy New York State Historical Association, Cooperstown.

Some of the most colorful paintings were done in watercolor on paper or silk. These memorials have a particular charm because of their gay hues. Watercolor was frequently used even when it was not the primary medium. Watercolor skies appear in the background of embroidered pictures, and charming watercolor faces were sometimes pasted or sewn on. At times as many as four different media or techniques were combined in a single picture.

Beatrix Rumford, in "Memorial Watercolors," comments on the difference in attitude between people today and people in preceding centuries:

> We tend to deny death by ignoring it and segregating the experience from everyday life. No modern schoolgirl would make a memorial to a departed relative. Our ancestors' handmade mourning pictures and other mortuary trappings may seem touching and

rather absurd but they interest the modern social historian because they are material evidence that the need to be remembered was an important aspect of death in the period when these mementos were popular, and suggest that earlier Americans were far more realistic about death than we are.

11

SOME EARLY CURES
AND REMEDIES

Arthritis

Carry a raw potato as near to the painful spot as possible; after three or four days the potato will dry up and the pain will disappear.

Let honeybees sting you, and when the stings have gone, so will your arthritis be gone.

Asthma

Lay the furry side of the pelt of a muskrat on the chest to make breathing easier.

Baldness

Boil rosemary tops in water, strain, apply vigorously to scalp to stimulate hair.

Eat parsnips daily to prevent baldness.

Pour rum on the head to ensure against baldness.

Rub an onion on the top of the head to make hair grow.

To keep hair from falling out, thoroughly wet the hair once or twice daily with a solution of salt and water.

Buffalo oil will prevent hair from falling out, make it grow faster, and improve its beauty.

Birthmarks

To remove, rub them with the hand of a corpse.

Boils

Boil flaxseed and apply warm.

Apply sugar and yellow soap.

Grate a raw potato, pat on boil, and wrap in cloth; after three days the boil will be gone.

Burns

Apply either a handful of flour or the yellow of an egg beaten into linseed oil with a feather; bind.

Chapped hands

Scrape beeswax lightly into a small widemouthed bottle until it is nearly filled; add a small piece of mutton tallow and fill with olive oil; set bottle on back of stove, and when wax is melted, add twelve drops of attar of roses.

Chicken pox

To cure, go out to the chicken house after the sun goes down, lie down, and let a black hen fly over you.

Colds

Place a mixture of onion and butter on the throat and chest.

Cook sliced onions in lard until hot and clear; place onions in a muslin bag and wear around neck until congestion is gone.

Pare the rind of an orange, roll it inside out, and place a roll in each nostril.

To keep children free from colds, tie a big red onion to the bedpost.

To make cough syrup, boil goldenrod and add sugar and peppermint syrup.

Diphtheria

Remove the fluid from the stool of a cow in the morning out in the pasture; collect enough to gargle with.

Earache

Dip cotton in molasses and put in the ear, and the pain will cease.

Place the juice of an onion in the ear to relieve pain.

A drop of white oil in the ear and a hot bed-warming pan under a pillow will cure the ache.

To cure a baby's earache, feed him bone marrow from a hog.

Eyes

Bathe the eyes in the water of the first rainfall in May to make them stronger; save the water for use during the year on sore or tired eyes.

The eyes of an owl placed on eyelids will cure blindness.

For sore eyes, place damp rose petals on eyelids.

To cure a sty, take nine prickers from a rose bush, touch the sty with eight, and throw ninth over your right shoulder, and the sty will disappear.

Fever

To reduce fever, swallow a spider with syrup.

To make a fever drink, pour cold water on wheat bran, let boil for half an hour, strain, and add sugar and lemon juice. Then pour boiling water on flaxseed and let stand until it is ropy; pour into lemonade, and drink.

Slice up a large quantity of onions and bind them on the soles of the feet of someone with a high fever to reduce the fever.

Headache

Dry and powder some moss; take as snuff to cure headache.

Hiccups

Drink water through a folded handkerchief.

Lice

To cure a head of lice, wash the head with whiskey and sand; the lice will get drunk with whiskey and, thinking that they are on sand, will fight each other to the death.

Lockjaw

Take a small quantity of turpentine, warm it, and pour it on the wound; relief will follow in less than a minute.

Nosebleed

To stop the bleeding, pour cold water down the victim's neck.

Place a puffball in nostril to stop bleeding.

Drill a hole in nutmeg and wear it in the hollow of your neck.

Poison ivy

Rub touch-me-nots on the sores; by morning the sores will start to go away. If not, rub a little more touch-me-nots on them.

Quinsy

To cure, tie a black cord around the neck.

Rashes

Rub parsley on the affected areas.

Rheumatism

To cure, smear the wrists with molasses and cover with brown paper.

Smallpox

Cure smallpox in three days by dissolving one ounce of cream of tartar in a pint of water, and take it at intervals.

Sore throat

Slice a thin piece of old smoked bacon, the older the better; stitch it to a piece of flannel and make it black with pepper; warm it and fasten it closely around the throat. Do not remove until the inflammation has been drawn to the outside. When the meat has been removed, anoint the throat with vaseline and bind up in flannel until well.

To relieve sore throat put a few drops of kerosine on a teaspoon of sugar and swallow it slowly.

Stomach disorders and indigestion

Carefully brown dry flour in a pan, then add water to make a thin gruel. Drink it to relieve digestive disorders.

Take a big drink of warm salt water; it will induce vomiting and get rid of the trouble.

Toothache

Gunpowder and brimstone will help ease the ache.

Fresh cow manure placed on the side of the face will draw out the pain of a toothache.

SOME EARLY CURES AND REMEDIES

Take a sliver of a pine tree that has been hit by lightning and prick the aching tooth with it to cure pain.

Warts

Cut a potato in half and rub it on the wart; bury the potato, and as it rots, so will the wart.

Bury a one-year-old clean dishcloth the same distance behind the barn as the height of the person who has the warts; wrap the warts for five days; then dig up the dishcloth and clean it, and the warts will be gone.

Spit on the wart every morning.

Rub a grain of barley on your wart, then feed the barley to a chicken.

Take cobwebs and roll them into little balls; place the cobwebs on the warts and set fire to them; let the fire burn down to the wart and then the wart will be gone. (It may leave a scar, but the wart will be gone.)

Sell your wart to someone for a penny.

12

EPITAPHS

A sampling, reflecting eighteenth- and nineteenth-century views, moral, religious, and humorous, on death and life.

Reader behold! and shed a tear
Think on the dust that slumbers here,
And when you read the fate of me,
Think on the glass that runs for thee.

A prudent wife is from the Lord.

Hark from the lambs a doleful sound
Mine ears attend the cry,
Ye living man come view the ground
Where you must shortly lie.

Happy Infant early blessed
Best in peacefull slumber rest,
Early rescued from his cares
Which increase with growing years.

Death is a debt to nature due
Which I have paid
And so must you.

DEATH IN EARLY AMERICA

In the midst of life we are in death.

The pains of death are past
Labor and sorrow cease.

The just intermingle in this cemetery.

Kind and affectionate
Gone to dwell with kindred spirits.
Amiable and obliging
Her guileless life
Endears her memory.

Behold and see as you pass by,
As you are now so once was I.
As I am now so you must be
Prepare for death and follow me.

Thou shalt come to thy grave
in a full age
as a field of corn
cometh in his season.

The earthly parents loved thee well,
So much that language fails to tell,
But oh, our love was weak and poor;
Thy Heavenly Parent loves thee more.

She loved people, these hills, and truth.

Go home dear Friends,
Lament no more
Am not lost
Am gone before.

In him lived integrity and kindness born of wisdom.

Certain name, thou hast left me,
here thy loss I deeply feel;
but 'tis God that hath bereft me,
he can all my sorrow heal.

EPITAPHS

An honest man is the noblest work of God.

Soft was the moment and serene.
That all her sufferings closed.
No agony nor struggle seen,
nor feature discomposed.

This the fair flower with
blooming beauties around
Cut down in the morn,
lies withering on the ground.

The sweet remembrance of the just
Shall flourish while they sleep in dust.

O cruel Death! how could you be so unkind,
To take him before and leave me behind?
You should have taken both of us if either
Which would have been more pleasing to the survivor.

Is this the fate, that all must die
will death no ages spare?
Then let us to Jesus go and
seek for refuge there.

Weep not around his cold clay bed,
Nor heave a mournful sigh,
For O! father's spirit fled
To realms above the sky.

Within the gloomy mansion of the Lord.

Shed not for her the bitter tear
Nor give the heart to vain regret
'Tis but the casket that lies here
The gem that filled it sparkles yet.

Lord Jesus may early death
Spread an alarm abroad
And may the youth in time of health
Prepare to meet their God.

DEATH IN EARLY AMERICA

She faithfully fulfilled the duties of the
several relations of life, in which she
was placed; and died in hope of a glorious
and blessed reward in the kingdom of her REDEEMER.

Farewell, bright soul, a short farewell;
till we shall meet again above
by the sweet groves where pleasure dwells,
and trees of life bear fruits of love.

Blessed are the dead which die in the Lord.

Her mind was tranquil and serene
No terrors in her looks were seen:
Her Savior's smile dispelled her gloom,
And smoothed her passage to the tomb.

What hopes lie buried here.

When the archangel's trump shall sound,
And souls to bodies Join,
What crowds shall wish their lives below
Had been as short as mine.

A loving Husband, a friend most dear
A tender partner lies here
In love we lived, in peace he died
His life was craved but God denied.

Little Hattie was our darling
Pride of all our hearts at home
But the angels came and called
Came and whispered Hattie come.

Sometime we'll understand.

Call not back the dear departed
Anchored safe where storms are o'er
On the border land we left him
Soon to meet and part no more.

EPITAPHS

My Lord hath called and I obeyed
To meet and with Him dwell
The last great debt I now have paid
And bid the world farewell.

Dear little sufferer once so brisk and gay
By sharp disease we saw thee pine away
Short was thy stay within this land of tears
And few the number of thy fleeting years.

He sleeps a youthful hero
With the honor of a soldier brave
Who gave up home, friends, and life itself
Our country still to save.

Here is rest for the weary
Here is rest for me.

BIBLIOGRAPHY

Primary sources

Baldwin, Charles, *Journals* of, New York State Library, Albany, N.Y.

Frary, Dr. Robert, *Ledger* of, New York State Library, Albany, N.Y.

Rockwell, Dr. S. R., *Diary* of, Connecticut State Library, Hartford, Conn.

Scott, Dr. Thomas, and Charlotte Wray. *Letters.* Collection of author.

Van Dyck, Dr. Cornelius, *Account Book* of, New York State Library, Albany, N.Y.

Warner, Dr. Richard, *Notebook* of, Connecticut State Library, Hartford, Conn.

Watrous, Dr. John, *Account Book* of, Connecticut State Library, Hartford, Conn.

Webster, Dr. Joshua, *Account Book* of, New York State Library, Albany, N.Y.

Books and magazine articles

Andrews, Edward Deming, *The People Called Shakers.* New York: Oxford University Press, 1953.

Bauer, W. W., *Potions, Remedies and Old Wives' Tales.* Garden City, N.Y.: Doubleday, 1969.

Berkey, Andrew S., *Practitioner of Physick: A Biography of Abraham Wagner, 1717–1763*. Pennsburg, Pa.: Schwenkfelder Library, 1954.

Bixler, Miriam Eyde, "Early Lancaster County Funeral Customs." *Journal of the Lancaster County Historical Society*. Vol. 77, No. 4, 1973.

Blackington, Alton, *Yankee Yarns*. New York: Dodd, Mead, 1954.

Blakeley, Phyllis R., *Nova Scotia's Two Remarkable Giants*. Windsor, Nova Scotia: Lancelot Press, 1970.

Buchan, Dr. William, *Domestic Medicine*. Boston: Otis, Broaders & Co., 1848.

Carson, Gerald, *Rum and Reform in Old New England*. Sturbridge, Mass.: Old Sturbridge Village, 1966.

Cist, Charles, *The Cincinnati Miscellany*. Cincinnati: Caleb Clark, 1845.

Dow, George F., *Everyday Life in the Massachusetts Bay Colony*. Boston: Society for the Preservation of Antiquities, 1935.

Earle, Alice Morse, *Colonial Days in Old New York*. New York: Charles Scribner & Sons, 1915.

Eberlein, Harold, and McClure, Abbott, *The Practical Book of Early American Arts and Crafts*. Philadelphia: J. B. Lippincott, 1916.

Emrich, Duncan, *It's an Old Wild West Custom*. New York: Vanguard Press, 1949.

Eyde, Abner McMichael, as told to Miriam Eyde Bixler, "A Lancaster City Boy in the Gay Nineties." *Journal of the Lancaster County Historical Society*. Vol. 77, No. 4.

Felt, Joseph B., *The Customs of New England*. Boston: T. R. Marvin, 1853.

Fletcher, Stevenson Whitcomb, *Pennsylvania Agriculture and Country Life*. Harrisburg: Pennsylvania Historical and Museum Commission, 1950.

Flexner, James T., *Doctors on Horseback and Pioneers of American Medicine*. New York: Dover Books, 1969.

Forbes, Harriette Merrifield, *Gravestones of Early New England*

and the Men Who Made Them, 1653–1800. Boston: Houghton Mifflin, 1927.

Gardner, Emelyn Elizabeth, *Folklore from the Schoharie Hills.* Ann Arbor: University of Michigan Press, 1937.

Garrett, Wendall, "The Price Books of the District of Columbia Cabinetmakers, 1831." *Antiques.* May 1975.

Gillon, Edmund V., *Early New England Gravestone Rubbings.* New York: Dover Books, 1966.

Gridley, Ella, *Few Are Left to Know.* Norwich, N.Y.: Chenango County Historical Society, 1970.

Haberstein, Robert W., and William M. Lamers, *The History of American Funeral Directing.* Milwaukee: Bullin Printers, 1955.

Hall, William M., *Reminiscences and Sketches*, Harrisburg, Pa.: Meyers Printing House, 1890.

Hedrick, Ulysses, *History of Agriculture in the State of New York.* Albany: New York State Agricultural Society, 1933.

Holloway, Laura C., *The Ladies of the White House.* Philadelphia: Bradley & Co., 1884.

Hostetler, John, *Amish Society.* Baltimore: Johns Hopkins Press, 1963.

Hunt, Thomas, *Wedding Days of Former Times.* Philadelphia: Griffith & Simon, 1845.

Jacobs, G. Walker, *Stranger, Stop and Cast an Eye.* Brattleboro, Vt.: The Stephen Greene Press, 1973.

Kane, Harnett T., *Gentlemen, Swords and Pistols.* New York: Ballantine Books, 1951.

Kelley, Joseph J., Jr., *Life and Times in Colonial Philadelphia.* Harrisburg, Pa.: Stackpole Books, 1973.

Klees, Fredric, *The Pennsylvania Dutch.* New York: Macmillan, 1950.

Kuhns, Oscar, *German and Swiss Settlements of Pennsylvania.* New York: Henry Holt & Co., 1900.

Lichten, Frances, *Decorative Art of Victoria's Era.* New York: Charles Scribner's Sons, 1950.

————. *Folk Art of Rural Pennsylvania*. New York: Charles Scribner's Sons, 1946.

Ludwig, Allan I., *Graven Images*. Middletown, Conn.: Wesleyan University Press, 1966.

Menchin, Robert S., *The Last Caprice*. New York: Simon & Schuster, 1963.

Mitford, Jessica, *The American Way of Death*. New York: Simon & Schuster, 1963.

Mussey, June Barrows, ed., *We Were New England*. New York: Stackpole Sons, 1937.

O'Callaghan, E. B., *The Documentary History of New York*. Vol. 3. Albany, N.Y.: Weed, Parson & Co., 1850.

Palmer, Henry Robinson, *Stonington-by-the-sea*. Palmer Press, 1913.

Pennell, Joseph, and others, *Quaint Corners in Philadelphia*. Philadelphia: John Wanamaker, 1922.

Pennsylvania Magazine of History and Biography. Vols. 5, 12, 17.

Rawson, Marion Nicholl, *Of the Earth Earthy*. New York: E. P. Dutton, 1937.

————. *Candleday Art*. New York: E. P. Dutton, 1938.

Riznik, Barnes, *Medicine in New England 1790–1840*. Sturbridge, Mass.: Old Sturbridge Village, 1965.

Rumford, Beatrix T., "Memorial Watercolors." *Antiques*. October 1973.

Samson, Harold E., *The Tug Hill Country*. Boonville, N.Y.: Willard Press, 1971.

Sandrof, Ivan, "As I am now so must you be." *American Heritage*. February 1960.

Sargent, L. M., *Dealings with the Dead*. Vols. 1 and 2. Boston: Dutton & Wentworth, 1855.

Sparks, Jared, *Sparks' American Biography*. Boston: Charles Little & James Brown, 1851.

Spinney, Frank O., "William S. Gookin, Portrait Painter of Dover, N.H." *Old Time New England*. Vol. 34, No. 4.

BIBLIOGRAPHY

Stoddard, Donald, "After the Hearse, Roumanian Verse." *Signature.* November 1974.

Sweeney, Edward J., "The Bussey Bridge Disaster." *Yankee Magazine.* March 1975.

Todd, Reverend John, "The Skeleton of Cranberry Lake." *The Adirondack Reader.* New York: Macmillan, 1964.

Van Voorhis, John S., *The Old and the New Monongahela.* Baltimore: Genealogical Publishing Co., 1974.

Walsh, William S., *Curiosities of Popular Customs.* Philadelphia: J. B. Lippincott, 1898.

Weygandt, Cornelius, *The Red Hills.* Philadelphia: University of Pennsylvania Press, 1929.

Wharton, Anne Hollingsworth, *Colonial Days and Dames.* Philadelphia: J. B. Lippincott, 1898.

———. *Social Life in the Early Republic.* Philadelphia: J. B. Lippincott, 1902.

Wigginton, Eliot, ed., *Foxfire 2.* Garden City, N.Y.: Doubleday, 1973.

Williams, Jean Webb, "Graveyarding in Old Schoharie." *Schoharie County Historical Review.* Vol. 32, No. 2.

Willis, N. P., *Rural Letters.* Auburn: Alden & Beardsley, 1856.

Wright, Richardson, *Hawkers and Walkers.* Philadelphia: J. B. Lippincott, 1927.

Young, John H., *Our Deportment.* Detroit: F. B. Dickerson, 1881.

Tapes

Alton Blackington. "Yankee Yarns." Broadcast over Boston radio station WBZ in the 1950s. Provided by John Furman.

Thesis

Rumford, Beatrix T. *The Role of Death as Reflected in the Art and Folkways of the Northeast in the Eighteenth and Nineteenth Centuries.* New York State Historical Association Library, Cooperstown, N.Y.

INDEX

G

H

INDEX

Hearts on gravestones, 176
Hen crow, warning of, 60
Herb doctors, 23
Hiccups, cure for, 221
Hiller, Dr. Henry, coffin of, 110
Holmes, Thomas, and embalming, 82
Home cures, 23, 24
Horse, warning of white, 60
Horses for hearses, use of, 118
Hospitality, funeral, 87
Hospitals, condition of, 21
House, Moravian corpse, 90
House Amish cemeteries, 135

I

Illness, causes of, 37
Illusion, warning of, 62
Indian wars, death rate from, 20
Indigestion, remedy for, 222
Inoculation, opposition to, 30
Invitations, funeral, 69, 71
Inviter, funeral, 69
Irish Catholics, funeral customs of, 85
Iron fences, 153

J

Jewelry
    as death gifts, 93
    hair mourning, 206
    mourning, 199

K

Killing, legal, 20
Knives, warning of crossed, 60

L

Laying out the dead, 81
Legal killing, 20

M

N

T